THE RANGITANE RIDDLE

A true maritime mystery

Trevor Bell

Birchfield Press

The Rangitane Riddle

First hardback edition printed 2012 in the United Kingdom.
A catalogue record for this book is available from the British Library.

ISBN 978-0-9572841-0-4

Published by Birchfield Press
Keeper's Lodge, Aston Lane, Hope Valley, S33 6SA, UK
01433 620962
enquiries@birchfield-press.co.uk

Designed and set by Trevor Bell
Artwork by Lucy Webster

Printed and bound in the UK by the MPG Books Group,
Bodmin and King's Lynn

Dedicated to

Frank Ellison
1920 - 2012

Contents

Preface

Frank Ellison was a young cabin steward on RMS *Rangitane* when it was intercepted and sunk off New Zealand in 1940. He was taken prisoner and, after many months, arrived in a POW camp in Germany, where he spent the remainder of the war.

Frank was my uncle by marriage and I vaguely knew that he had been a POW but, like many millions of people who experienced the trauma of war, he rarely spoke of his experience. In his eighties, he started reminiscing and wondered what had happened to Johnny Thompson, his best friend from *Rangitane* with whom he shared a POW camp hut for four years. I sat Frank in front of my computer and quickly found on the internet a photograph of him and Johnny in the camp. Frank then started telling me the amazing story of *Rangitane*: I was hooked!

I have learnt that research is not easy when the subject is fascinating. I spent too long exploring new worlds which, while absolutely absorbing to me, made me wander from the main line of my research. As a result, and to my regret, Frank died only a few months before this book was published. I would have loved to have presented it to him.

Trevor Bell
May 2012

Acknowledgements

I am indebted to many dozens of people who have contacted and helped me since I first set up a web site about *Rangitane*. The majority are relatives of the crew and passengers who were on her fateful final voyage. I am pleased to include in this book their family stories and personal anecdotes which have turned a factual commentary into a truly human story.

I am particularly grateful to Captain Upton's family who gave me a copy of his personal notes and the parole agreement referred to in Chapter 12.

A significant amount of new research material came to light in 2008, when the long-suffering Archives New Zealand finally located the original proceedings of a 1941 Commission of Inquiry. This had been set up to investigate allegations of subversion which may have led to the capture of *Rangitane* and six other ships. I am grateful to that service and to the Australian Archives, the UK National Archives, Imperial War Museum and the National Maritime Museum for material which has led to a definitive account of the events in 1940.

Finally, I must pay public tribute to my wife, Christine, who has been a research-widow for far too long. She has taken her revenge while proof-reading the book by proving that her grammar and spelling are far superior to mine. I am originally from Somerset and she accuses me of writing with a Somerset dialect. If there are any lingering errors, I apologise: they are definitely mine, not hers.

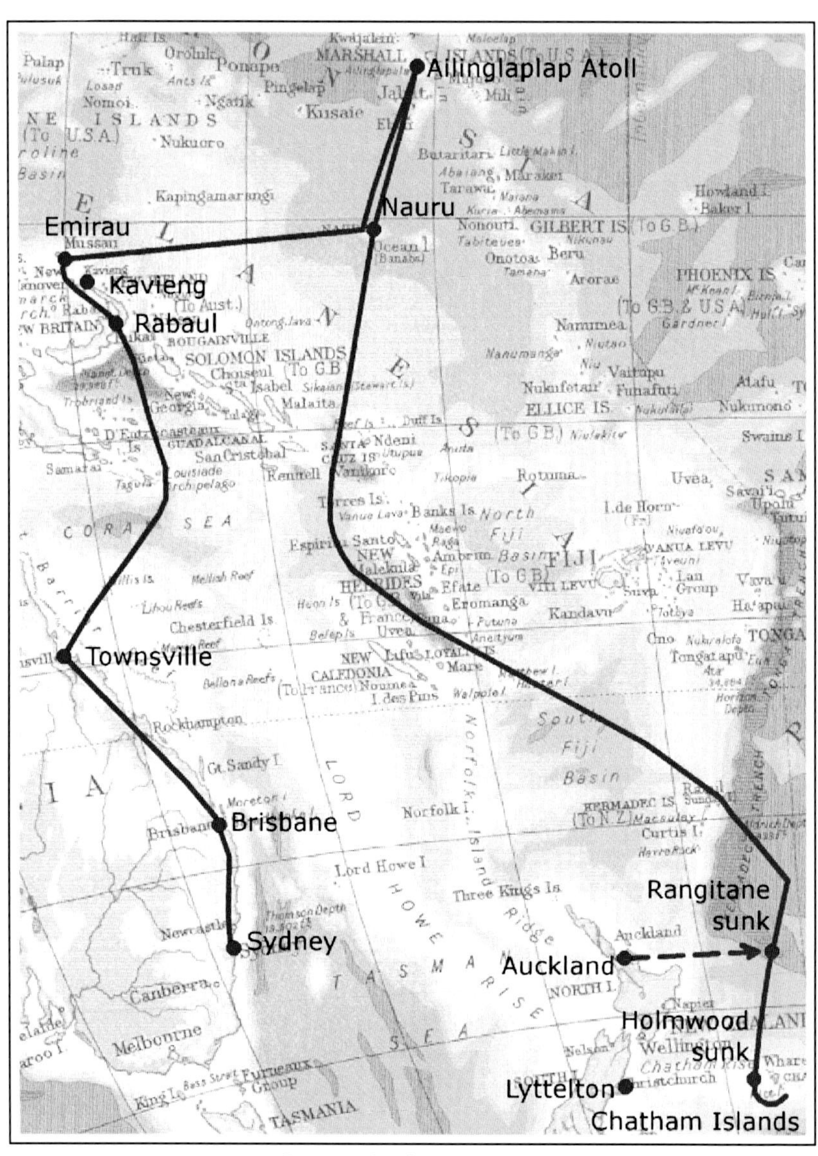

Journey taken by Rangitane's survivors

RANGITANE.

Introduction

The Royal Mail Ship *Rangitane* was a large, fast, majestic, two-funnelled ocean liner; an icon of the golden age of sea travel. Early in the Second World War she was intercepted and sunk by two small, slow, scruffy German raiders disguised as Japanese merchant traders, far from the main theatre of war. Why and how did this happen? Was it true that they knew where to find *Rangitane*? Were there really secret agents feeding the Germans with information? Had British secret codes been compromised? Why did the raiders sail over a thousand miles out of their way to release the majority of the survivors on a remote British island while others were shipped back to POW camps in Germany? This is the Rangitane Riddle.

Waging war against merchant ships is as old as warfare itself. Germany had learnt in the First World War that Britain's greatest weakness was that she was an island dependent on imports of food to feed her people and raw materials for her industries. While the two nations' bigger capital ships were effectively confined to their anchorages in that war, Germany was successful against British merchant shipping using lone warship raiders to lay mines in shipping lanes and to sink or capture easy targets. The raiders initially consisted of six light battle cruisers which were already at sea on the outbreak of the Great War. Two of these, the *Emden* and *Karlsruhe,* claimed the majority of the 200,000 tons of shipping sunk by all of the cruisers. These raiders were supplemented by several larger armed liners whose speed allowed them to outrun even the fastest warship, but their success was limited by the logistics of feeding their ravenous appetites for coal.

One year into the First World War it became evident that warships and liners were too easily identifiable and too difficult to re-provision at long range. A more cunning strategy was needed. It had been proved that small, innocuous-looking merchant vessels were ideal as minelayers despite their relative slowness. A young naval officer, Theodor Wolff, proposed that similar vessels should be heavily armed under a merchant trader disguise. He argued that their large cargo holds could be filled with enough coal to allow long periods of independent operation at sea and that their innocent look, often taking on the identity of a neutral country, and their ability to change outward appearance would give them the benefit of stealth and surprise. An ordinary-looking 4,800 ton banana ship was converted into the *Moewe,* armed with four 5.9-inch guns, one 4.1-inch gun, two torpedo tubes and 500 mines. This went on to capture or sink over forty ships during fifteen months at sea. Wolff's point had been proved and other armed merchant raiders, or *Hilfskreuzer*, followed, notably *Emden* and *Seeadler*, commanded by Karl von Muller and Count Felix von Luckner respectively. Both commanders became heroes at home for their daring exploits and became the stuff of legend for years to come.

The Treaty of Versailles severely limited Germany's post-war navy to no more than a token force of outdated warships, no submarines and no military aircraft and she lost the majority of her overseas territories suitable for naval bases. But secret plans were already being laid as early as 1927 by the increasingly confident Weimar Republic, to rearm its forces and to provide a support network with the more sympathetic countries on the furthest reaches of the oceans. After Hitler came to power, plans were made to build four auxiliary cruisers based on the same principles as the successful raiders from the previous war. Admiral Erich Raeder, the German Commander-in-Chief, believed that long-distance raiders working independently with little support were the best way of attacking merchant ships in the absence of overseas naval bases. But Raeder had to compete with the demands of the army and air force for scarce resources and the four raiders were never built. Germany's rearmament focussed on Hitler's belief that the coming war would be fought on land and in the air; part of his logic was that merchant ships could be obliterated if the *Luftwaffe* dominated the skies around Britain. Raeder was also told that there would be no need for a large scale naval fleet until 1945.

When the war began in 1939, the *Kriegsmarine* were totally ill-prepared, having only two pocket battleships and a handful of U-boats at war readiness, although many more warships were in preparation. But the lack of auxiliary cruisers based on the successful First World War model was frustrating, so orders were placed in November 1939 to convert twelve merchant vessels into fully-fledged *Hilfskreuzer*. The work took longer than expected; a severe winter, material shortages and diversion of effort to support land forces all contrived to delay the work by three months.

The first raider to be completed was *Atlantis*, followed soon after by *Orion*. Eight others later set sail, but one never made it to the open sea and two of the original twelve never left the shipyard. The scale of the task of converting and provisioning raiders was daunting. The merchant ships chosen for conversion varied between 3,300 and 7,800 tons with large cargo holds. They had to be strengthened to withstand the recoil of six 5.9-inch guns hidden behind false bulwarks, modified to launch torpedoes, lay mines and to launch and recover a seaplane. A significant amount of space was reserved to accommodate prisoners and, by 1940s standards, a modern operating theatre. As a normal merchant ship there would have been about forty crewmen; as an auxiliary raider there were as many as four hundred including specialist code breakers, surgeons, linguists and intelligence officers. The stores had to be sufficient for a totally independent floating village and even included clothing for women prisoners.

By mid-1940 there were six raiders at sea causing problems for allied shipping. Their ability to travel unnoticed under neutral flags and to change disguise meant that the British had little idea of how many raiders there were, where their areas of operations lay and what they looked like. The warfare was not just the sinking or capturing of allied merchant ships: the raiders wrought intelligence confusion by sometimes pretending to be *Kriegsmarine* warships, sending panic down the Admiralty's corridors. Germany's *Ettapendeinst*, or secret logistics support service, ensured that individual raiders were supported and re-provisioned for periods of over one year even in the farthest oceans. In 1940, Japan was already providing logistical support and intelligence updates to surface raiders although she had yet to enter the war. *Seekriegsleitung*, or SKL, Germany's naval control service, nominally controlled the raiders but in practice each commander had considerable discretion on tactics. There was minimal radio contact between SKL and individual raiders and commanders often became frustrated at seemingly ridiculous orders from desk-bound SKL staff totally out of touch with the current situation at sea.

In July 1940 a new section was set up in the British Admiralty's Operational Intelligence Centre to try to make sense of what was happening with the raiders. It was a long and painstaking process of intelligence analysis, particularly from survivor debriefing, and it was not until May 1941 that weekly intelligence reports could be made with any accuracy about the names, description and location of raiders. Some of the data came from agents in neutral ports where raider and U-boat supply ships were provisioned. These ships, often captured allied merchant vessels, would re-provision raiders at pre-arranged locations and would exchange crew, deliver secret orders and collect war diaries and captured intelligence material for onward delivery to Berlin.

Between mid-1940 and late-1943 the nine auxiliary cruisers were surprisingly successful: they operated in the Atlantic, Pacific and Indian Oceans, reaching as far as the Antarctic. They sank nearly 900,000 tons of shipping, three times the tonnage of that sunk by surface warships and at a fraction of the cost to the *Kriegsmarine*. Hitler was always furious when one of his highly prized capital ships was lost, despite their relative effectiveness. One can question whether he even knew when each of eight *Hilfskreuzer* was lost to enemy action.

There have been many books and memoirs published on auxiliary cruisers. While many give a factual account of their strategic impact, others are very personal accounts from their victims. This book combines the two narratives: it looks at the circumstance and consequences, nationally and personally, of the sinking of one particular ship, the RMS *Rangitane,* by two raiders working together with their supply ship in the South Pacific in November 1940. As already noted, this was a time when British naval intelligence had no idea how many German raiders were at sea, what they were, where they were and how they were operating. The significance, at the time, of this particular incident is that many of the survivors were convinced that the Germans knew exactly where to find *Rangitane* and that secret information was being released in New Zealand. The British, Australian and New Zealand authorities were thrown into turmoil, resulting in an official inquiry which looked at the whole question of security surrounding merchant shipping. Many people, with benefit of hindsight, will claim that the incident was no different to the thousands of similar losses in the maritime war. At the time, and to the individuals affected, it was all very personal.

Chapter 1

The end of the story

In January 1964, Lionel Upton was enjoying a quiet retirement at home in Hove, Sussex. At seventy-eight years old, he had good reason to be satisfied with his life. He had served at sea during two world wars and had been the dedicated servant of only one employer in all his working life – the New Zealand Shipping Company. Lionel received a surprise letter from an ex-colleague in Australia. Enclosed with the letter was a recent newspaper cutting from the Rockhampton Morning Gazette in Queensland. It showed a photograph of a teenager holding a section of what had originally been a circular lifebelt, and described how he found it wedged in rocks while on a fishing trip in Crocodile Bay, ninety miles north of Rockhampton. Evidently old and long forgotten, the relic still showed in large faded letters the name of the ship it came from: *RANGITANE.*

Nobody in the Rockhampton area would remember a ship called *Rangitane*, but Captain Herbert Lionel Upton, DSC, RD, ADC, RNR, reading the cutting, certainly did. He immediately wrote to thank his ex-colleague for sending it and in doing so recalled how it all started twenty-four years previously. He finished his letter with 'Poor old Tane' (his nickname for *Rangitane*) 'I have very happy memories of her and always regret her end.'

The story that ended in Crocodile Bay started over two thousand miles away in Auckland, New Zealand, in the dark days of the Second World War.

Chapter 2

The beginning of the story

The RMS (Royal Mail Ship) *Rangitane* was built on the Upper Clyde, Glasgow as hull number 522 by John Brown & Co. Ltd. and launched on Monday 27 May, 1929. She was the last of three sister '*Rangi*' ships built for the London registered New Zealand Shipping Company (NZSC) - the others were the *Rangitiki* and *Rangitata;* individually they were nick-named *Tane, Tiki* and *Tata* and all came into service in 1929. The *Rangi* ships were known as refrigerated cargo-liners; each was 16,700 tons and could carry nearly 600 passengers, 200 crew and thousands of tons of cargo and were built specifically for England-New Zealand run. They were the first diesel powered NZSC ships, having twin propellers powered by Brown Sulzer diesel engines with a total output of 9,300 HP.

An NZSC ship departed every fourth Thursday from London for New Zealand, making the journey in thirty-five days via the Panama Canal. Each ship operated a regular cycle of twenty weeks between departures. Following five weeks at sea it took four weeks to offload and load cargo in New Zealand, five weeks to return and six weeks to offload and reload cargo in England for the next round trip. In normal service, *Rangitane* could carry 100 first-class passengers, 80 second-class and 410 third-class. She had been re-fitted in 1935, particularly to increase her refrigeration capacity to carry more dairy and meat products. The service ran regularly from 1929 until 1939, initially leaving from Plymouth but from the mid-1930s from the King George

V dock in the east end of London. The NZSC was represented in the UK by J B Westray & Co Ltd who had their offices near Blackwall pier from where their sailing ships had departed at the end of the previous century. After the outbreak of war, when the mouth of the Thames had been mined and London was within range of enemy bombers, departures were transferred to Liverpool. The war curtailed the regular service but the *Rangi* ships continued to sail under requisition to the Ministry of Shipping, later named the Ministry of War Transport. This often included the familiar trips to New Zealand but also involved the dreaded Atlantic run operating as troop ships.

Rangitane had sailed from Liverpool bound for Wellington, New Zealand in September, 1940 but the start of the journey had been disrupted. She had cast-off at 6.30 a.m. on 25 September to meet up with convoy OB219, consisting of twenty-five merchant ships and four naval protection escorts. She was ordered to return to Liverpool to discharge some of her passengers: they were 113 children and their supervisors who were being evacuated under a government scheme organised by the Children's Overseas Reception Board, commonly referred to as CORB. The scheme was intended to evacuate children from British cities suffering the Blitz to Canada, South Africa, Australia and New Zealand. The scheme had been operating throughout the summer of 1940 until 17 September when the *City of Benares* was torpedoed and sunk on its way to Canada. On board were ninety child

Excitable CORB evacuees ready to start a new life

evacuees, seventy-seven of whom died, together with six of the ten CORB escorts. When news reached the British public there was a huge outcry and a week of political dithering. Some evacuee ships were allowed to sail, some were not. *Rangitane* had already sailed with CORB Batch Z3 of 113 children on the morning of 25 September but was recalled that same day. The situation was so sensitive that *Rangitane* was escorted the short way back to Liverpool by *HMS Winchelsea*, a long range escort destroyer, and the children were eventually returned to their homes.

Rangitane finally set sail again later on 25 September, using her speed to catch up with convoy OB219. It had been compulsory since the start of the war for all ships sailing the dangerous Atlantic waters to be in an escorted convoy. Late 1940 was a time of spectacular success for U-boat wolf-packs, a period which was known as 'The Happy Time' by the German commanders. Between July and October 1940, the allies lost 270 merchant vessels and relatively few convoys escaped unscathed. Survival prospects were not good: Convoy 218 which sailed the day before *Rangitane* was to lose one-quarter of its complement to U-boats. But *Rangitane* and her sister convoy ships were relatively lucky on this occasion, losing only a small Dutch steamer which had straggled behind. The convoy sailed to a dispersal point south of Iceland and turned to make their individual way to their final destinations.

Rangitane arrived safely in New Zealand. In Wellington and Auckland she was loaded with thousands of tons of cargo - seven million pounds of butter, cheese, frozen lamb and pork, cocoa beans, wool, hides, barrels of oil and forty-five bars of silver, all destined for a grateful British public and valued at over £2 million at 1940 prices. It took three weeks to load *Rangitane,* much longer than usual because there was a labour strike in New Zealand. Many of the crew must have had their private thoughts and doubts about how many trips could be made running the risk of attack. While the passengers assumed that their greatest danger would be on the home run in the Atlantic, the officers knew that there had already been enemy activity in the south Pacific.

Five months earlier, the 13,000 ton RMS *Niagara* was sunk by a mine in the Hauraki Gulf, just a few miles from where *Rangitane* was berthed. She had been another beautiful two-funnelled John Brown ship and was a victim of an unknown mine layer. On the same day the Norwegian SS *Tropic Sea* disappeared, as did the SS *Notou* about four weeks later, neither of which had raised any warning signal. In August the SS *Turakina* encountered a German raider disguised as a merchant ship in the Tasman Sea and was sunk after a valiant battle, giving her time to send emergency messages to the naval authorities. HMNZS *Achilles*, a *Leander*-class light cruiser, was sent on a fruitless hunt for the enemy around the Campbell Islands in the south. She returned to Lyttelton to re-provision just as *Rangitane* was preparing to sail.

Boarding *Rangitane* on the weekend of 23 November were 111 passengers; groups of people brought together and travelling for all sorts of reasons, all out of necessity and none for pleasure. One group consisted of twenty-two CORB volunteers, nineteen of whom had escorted 477 child evacuees from Liverpool to Australia on the *SS Batory* - a requisitioned Polish ship. The volunteers included six nurses and a dentist, dietician, PT instructor and chaplain. After the war, two of these, Betsy Sandbach and Geraldine Edge wrote a book of their experiences. *Batory*'s journey from Liverpool to Sydney had started on 4 August, 1940, before the loss of the seventy-seven children on the *City of Benares*. Also on *Batory* were about 300 troops destined for the Far East. The

MS Batory - The Singing Ship

convoy of sixteen ships had travelled to Freetown, Cape Town, Bombay, Colombo and Singapore, before landing the children at Fremantle, Melbourne and Sydney. The journey had evidently been a happy one: there was so much music and laughter that *Batory* was dubbed the 'Singing Ship' and was the subject of another book by the same name. *Batory* delivered her precious cargo safely and left Sydney on 3 November destined for Wellington to collect and deliver New Zealand soldiers to the Middle East. As *Batory* would not return to Britain, some of the evacuee escorts had to travel on to New Zealand to join *Rangitane* for the return trip to England. Another three CORB escorts joined them from the *SS Nestor* which had left Liverpool sixteen days after *Batory* with a batch of eighty-two evacuees, together with four children who had been left behind by *Batory* in a stopover port by mistake! When they sailed from Sydney to Wellington the CORB escorts were described as feeling 'lost and lonely' without the children.

On *Rangitane* there were also twenty-five redundant Polish crew from *Batory*. Two of these were alleged to have been deserters from the Polish armed forces and were being repatriated, while five others had been dismissed from *Batory* because of laziness and insubordination. The two deserters are reported to have been escorted under guard from Sydney to Wellington. There were also sixteen crewmen returning to England from the *SS Baltannic* which had arrived from Liverpool in mid-November and was to stay in New Zealand as a coastal steamer.

Other passengers on *Rangitane* included a group of fifteen New Zealand recruits travelling in mufti for Fleet Air Arm training and another eighteen Royal New Zealand Air Force men. The RNZAF men included wireless operators trained at Wigram, pilot officers and three Auckland University graduates, Billy Harden, Harry (Kim) Kimberley and Ian Shaw, on their way to England to join a radar development team. In 1941, twenty of these airmen were to become known as the

'Rangitane Boys' in their POW camp. Three passengers were travelling to British Guiana in South America via Panama: one was Molly Black, a bride-to-be travelling with her trousseau; the other two were Mr. and Mrs. Stuart who were the only first-class passengers. William Stuart was a judge travelling to his new appointment in British Guiana and his wife, Starr, was described as a writer. Both were to become infamous for their disgraceful arrogance and conduct over the following weeks. Contrary to sensationalised reports in the press at the time, there were no children on *Rangitane*.

Captain Lionel Upton, DSC, RD, ADC, RNR had been the master of *Rangitane* for nearly two years. He was reported to have been a popular captain who had joined the New Zealand Shipping Company in 1902 as an apprentice from the training ship *Worcester*. In 1903 he became a Royal Naval Reservist and was called-up as an Acting Lieutenant for naval duty on the outbreak of the First World War. For most of the war he was in command of a group of armed trawlers and Q-boats protecting the naval fleet at Scapa Flow from U-boats. Q-boats were armed vessels disguised as simple traders or trawlers to lure German submarines to the surface. He was clearly successful: in 1917 he was awarded the Distinguished Service Cross 'for services in action with enemy submarines' and received a glowing letter of commendation from Admiral Sir Stanley Colville for the way he handled a particular incident. In the light of what was to happen to Upton and *Rangitane,* it is somewhat ironic that Upton had cut his teeth in command of deception ships. He later served on minesweepers in the English Channel for which he was awarded the French Legion of Honour medal.

Captain Herbert Lionel Upton

Following WW1, Upton served on New Zealand Shipping Company's training ships until taking over as master of *Rangitane* in early 1938. In 1939 he was promoted to Acting Commander in the Royal Navy Reserve and appointed ADC to King George VI. This was to be his last trip in command, having been called-up for naval duties. Upton was a devoted company man, describing the New Zealand Shipping Company as 'the best company in the land.' He was married and lived in Hove, Sussex. Before the outbreak of the Second World War his son followed in his father's footsteps, joining the company as a junior officer and later serving in the Indian Navy.

Upton was a relatively stocky man in his mid-fifties; one passenger described him as somebody who immediately commanded respect and exuded authority without being overbearing. His greatest vice was that he was a chain-smoker, something he was to rue in the weeks to come when tobacco was hard to come by. His crew was predominantly from Britain with some New Zealanders and Australians. On *Rangitane*'s final voyage there were 201 crew and only 111 passengers, a somewhat lopsided ratio of crew to passengers but a reflection of the fact that very few people wanted to travel voluntarily towards the main theatre of war. Captain Upton was preparing for his sixth voyage commanding *Rangitane* under wartime conditions. He was evidently very fond of his ship; in a letter in 1964 in which he mentions her loss, he said 'Poor old *Tane*. I have very happy memories of her and always regret her end.' His Chief Officer was Ernest 'Hoppy' Hopkins, who had trained in Liverpool and served in destroyers and submarine *K6* in WW1 based in Scapa Flow at the same time as Upton. There is no evidence that they ever knew each other at that time. He had joined the New Zealand Shipping Company in 1922 and had spent 17 years on the Australian and New Zealand runs before being made Upton's right-hand man.

Rangitane left her berth in Auckland harbour at 1 p.m. on Sunday 24 November, 1940 and sailed a short distance to anchor offshore in complete blackout for the night in Rangitoto Bay, in the lee of Mount Rangitoto. It is not clear why she anchored; it was unusual but there are two possible explanations. First, it may have been to allow minesweepers to check the channel because of incidents earlier in the year; or the more likely reason was that there was continuing paranoia about German sympathisers in New Zealand passing on information on shipping activities to the enemy. Laying up overnight would have thrown out the estimated position of *Rangitane* in the first few days. In his personal manuscript, Ernest Ball, a CORB chaplain, said that laying-up in Rangitoto Bay was not exactly a secret: the ship was regularly illuminated by shore-based searchlights checking the comings and goings during the night. At five o'clock on the Monday morning the anchor was weighed and *Rangitane* started on her familiar trip across the Pacific to the Panama Canal. Captain Upton had sailed the route many times but since the start of hostilities he was required to vary his course. He had received secret instructions on his transit to Panama from the Naval Control Service, whose responsibility it was to ensure that ships followed varying routes. Other restrictions meant that he had to maintain a blackout at night and strict radio silence at all times. *Rangitane* cleared the 'swept channel' by noon on 25 November.

Rangitane was a big passenger ship for her day. At 530 feet in length and nearly seventy feet in the beam, her cruising speed was sixteen knots. She would have been quite a majestic sight, particularly with her two funnels. But, like the fated *Titanic*, one funnel was a dummy, implying additional size and power. On the outbreak of war, *Rangitane*'s sleek profile was changed by the fitting of armament. There appears to be contradictory evidence about how she was armed: in his personal account and in evidence given in 1941, Captain Upton consistently referred only to 'the gun' and 'the gun platform', whereas German war diaries said that *Rangitane* had one 4.7-inch gun, another 60 mm gun and two 25 mm light American anti-aircraft guns on the wings of the bridge. Whatever the armament, it was more a psychological boost for the crew and passengers than a true means of defence. The arming of merchant ships was a contentious issue at the start of the war. Merchant seamen believed that they were civilians, not members of the armed forces, and that the Germans could claim merchant ships as legitimate targets if they were armed, no matter how lightly. However, many merchant ships received armament and trained Royal Navy or Army personnel to man the guns under the Defensively Equipped Merchant Ships (DEMS) scheme. In addition, many ships had mercantile crew who had received basic gun training. By the end of the war over 150,000 merchant seamen had received gunnery training. *Rangitane*'s 4.7-inch gun was manned by Royal Navy Volunteer Reservist George Wilson, Royal Navy Gunner Donald Windridge and Merchant Seamen/Gunners Clarence Henderson and A. Mills. Henderson is reported to have had four week's gun training but no experience under fire, but plenty of experience of being sunk: he was a survivor of the SS *Arandora Star*, a large passenger liner torpedoed only four months earlier while transporting German and Italian internees to Canada. Henderson was lucky to escape with his life because 713 of the 1299 internees and 92 of the 374 British crew and military guard perished.

Typical DEMS stern gun

Upton reported that the 4.7-inch gun had been fired with practice shots approximately twelve times since the start of the war, an average of four shots per round trip. No practice had been carried out on the final voyage because they had run out of practice ammunition. *Rangitane*'s total arsenal for the 4.7-inch gun was a meagre forty rounds of ammunition.

Chapter 3

The loss of the *Holmwood*

About two hours after *Rangitane* started her journey, a dramatic series of events was unfolding just off the Chatham Islands, a group of islands 400 miles to the east of New Zealand. The 247 ton coastal steamer *Holmwood* had set sail at 2.30 a.m. on the same day from Waitangi on the Chatham Islands for Lyttelton, 460 miles away on South Island near Christchurch and 500 miles from where *Rangitane* had started her journey. She was built in 1911 by the Goole Shipbuilding Company on the River Humber in Britain and had originally been named *Tees*. She had only recently been bought, extensively refurbished and renamed by the Holm Shipping Company of Wellington and was on only her second trip from the Chathams for her new owner. *Holmwood* was carrying twenty-nine passengers and crew, including four women and four children, 1370 sheep, two dogs and a horse. *Holmwood*'s captain was James Miller who had been on watch from leaving the Chathams in the early hours of the morning until changing shift with his second mate, Claude Clark, at 6.30 a.m. Miller retired to his bunk in his cabin next to the *Holmwood*'s bridge.

MV Holmwood

The full truth of the sequence of events a few hours later was difficult to ascertain but the consequences were to be so severe that an official inquiry would be set up in February, 1941. The inquiry was to take evidence into the circumstances surrounding the capture of *Holmwood* by German raiders and how it escalated into the loss of six more merchant ships in the region during the next two weeks. It was claimed that if *Holmwood*'s captain had raised the alarm on the mainland, *Rangitane* could have been recalled to port and shipping in the South Pacific could have been warned to be on their guard against three German raiders. Admiralty standing orders to all ships required that they must report unusual or suspicious sightings; the purpose was not necessarily to seek immediate help but to warn other ships and authorities of potential danger. However, it was generally accepted that if radio warnings were broadcast, enemy raiders would immediately attack the ship being stalked. The standard raider warning message was QQQQ for an armed merchant raider or RRRR for a warship raider, followed by the name of the ship sending the message and her position.

Miller was to be heavily criticised for not broadcasting a warning message; he later insisted that he was not roused in his cabin until 7.25 a.m. at the earliest when he found to his dismay a ship with Japanese markings about two miles off the port beam. He said that by the time he dressed and tried to read the ship's signals telling him to heave-to, it was too late to transmit the warning. He also claimed that his radio was not powerful enough to reach the Wellington radio station on the mainland and that there would be no radio operator on the nearby Chatham Islands until 9 a.m. He was to have no answer to the argument that there may have been other shipping in the region that may have picked up his transmission. Unfortunately, Second Mate Clark contradicted Miller by insisting that he had seen the first signs of a ship on the horizon just after 7 a.m. and had roused Miller at 7.10 a.m. when he became suspicious about the ship which was still five miles away. Miller disagreed, saying that Clark must have had the ship in view at least twenty-five minutes before rousing him at 7.25 a.m. Other members of the crew gave both supporting and contradicting evidence over the timings.

As it was, the ship with Japanese markings painted on the sides gained on *Holmwood*, suddenly dropped its sides to expose naval guns, covered the Japanese markings with Swastikas and raised international signal flags which Miller read as 'In the interests of your company you are to proceed to.' Miller was a little confused by the wording until a German officer later told him that the meaning 'In the interests of your ship's company you are to stop' became distorted in translation. The Germans also fired two warning shots, one across the bow and the other over bridge which Miller initially claimed he did not hear. 'Didn't you hear our shots?' asked the German. 'No, did you fire?' said Miller to which the German replied 'I thought you might not have seen it, it was only a small gun.' Miller was later to admit that he might have heard something, a story which he exaggerated out of all proportion when interviewed by the press two months later: he claimed that the shot over the bridge was so low that he had to duck his head to avoid being hit.

Miller said that he followed Admiralty orders by instructing Angus Campbell to throw all the ship's papers, Admiralty instructions and code books overboard in a weighted bag before signalling the engine room to stop engines. Just after 8 a.m. everyone on *Holmwood* was aware that they were encircled by three menacing ships, the one still in Swastika colours, the others in Japanese colours. Miller made sure that everybody was roused from their cabins. When he told Mrs McMahon, one of the passengers who was suffering

Holmwood being evacuated

badly with sea-sickness, that they had been caught by the Germans, she simply said 'Who cares?' and wanted to turn over and go back to sleep. Miller instructed his crew to put as many provisions and blankets into the lifeboats which were then lowered into the water. A pinnace arrived with a German officer and armed sailors who quickly established how many crew and passengers there were. They were surprised to find some women and children board; their intention had been to cast the occupants off to make their way back to the Chathams in the lifeboats, but the women and children wrong-footed them. After signalling his commander, the German officer told the survivors that they would be taken with the two dogs to the raider. They then started searching for papers and possessions and to see what they could salvage from the cargo. Fred Abernethy, *Holmwood*'s chief engineer, had two sporting rifles in his cabin which were found and confiscated. To his amazement, he was given a receipt for them with the promise that they were returned to him on his release. And they were, only four weeks later.

The alarm in New Zealand over *Holmwood* was not raised until the 27th November, a day after she was due to arrive in Lyttelton, but the shipping company had difficulty convincing the authorities that it was anything other than a mechanical breakdown. After air and sea searches over three days, the New Zealand Navy Office had to concede the worst. Prime Minister Peter Fraser sent telegrams to the families of the crew and passengers informing them that the loss may be the result of enemy raiders who were known to be in the area. Eventually the story hit the national press on 2nd December, a full week after the sinking. It would be another three weeks of worry before the families received another two telegrams from the Prime Minister to say that their loved-ones were safe and on their way home.

The three German raiders posing as Japanese merchant ships were the *Komet*, *Orion* and *Kulmerland*, disguised as the

Manyo Maru, *Maebasi Maru* and *Tokio Maru* respectively. *Komet* and *Orion* were true raiders – purposely converted merchant ships and heavily armed; *Kulmerland* was their unarmed supply ship. Their task was to search out allied merchant vessels in the south Pacific and to make such a nuisance of themselves that allied warships would be diverted away from the main theatre of war. They had been patrolling the south Pacific area in and around New Zealand for five weeks with no success. The two armed ships would sail each side of and just within sight of *Kulmerland*, thus enabling the squadron to cover an eighty mile tract of ocean. Their mission had been so unsuccessful that the raiders had decided to sail several thousand miles to the north and disrupt phosphate supply ships at the island of Nauru. Their route was to take them northwards between New Zealand and the Chatham Islands. On the night of Sunday 24 November they were south-west of the Chatham Islands sailing north. In his wartime diary Captain Eyssen of *Komet* noted how the current and wind had made them drift too close to the Chathams and they were near enough to see the lights on the islands. According to Eyssen, they saw smoke from a ship off the starboard bow sailing westwards. It was to be the *Holmwood.*

What *Komet*'s boarding party found on *Holmwood* was a delight. As well as some code books and ship's papers they found a sack of mail and records of wireless transmissions between the Chathams and the mainland which would keep their intelligence officers busy for weeks. But the main prize was fresh mutton. The boarding party took command of *Holmwood* with her crew and passengers and all four ships then set off on a course of 010º to try to clear the main shipping lane. It was not until 10.15 a.m. that they all stopped. Captain Miller and his crew and passengers were transferred to *Komet* where they contemplated an unknown fate. Six year old Julia McMahon, daughter of the Chatham Island's postmaster and wireless operator, was the youngest of the prisoners of war.

Eyssen recorded his opinion that his prisoners would probably enjoy their journey much more on *Komet* instead of sharing *Holmwood* with 'stinking sheep.' There then followed welcome additions to the raiders' stores: *Komet* received one hundred sheep, canned food, fruit and vegetables, together with *Holmwood's* radio, copies of radio transmissions and a number of navigation charts and code books. *Orion* received 200 live sheep and *Kulmerland* nineteen already slaughtered sheep.

Each of the three raiders took a *Holmwood* lifebelt as a memento of the event. Eyssen considered commandeering the *Holmwood* to become a minelayer but at a speed of eight to nine knots, she would not be able to keep up with the other raiders. He therefore decided to use *Holmwood* for live target practice - the first time his gunners had had the opportunity to display their skills since leaving Germany. After ensuring that the horse had been shot, Eyssen positioned *Komet* just over a mile away and attacked the *Holmwood* with the 5.9-inch starboard guns. Eyssen recorded that the range-finding was not good and the distance had to be reduced to less than half a mile before a successful hit below the water line was achieved. It took thirty minutes to despatch *Holmwood* to her grave, by which time the raiders could smell the stench of burning sheep carcasses.

Eyssen recorded his delight at having his first victim. The lack of any success had clearly been preying on his mind after so long at sea. 'The spell is broken' he wrote in his diary. 'I have had the patience to wait... the crew are clearly inspired.... this was not a large victim, but it is the beginning I wanted.'

In fact the German commanders could not believe how easily they had captured *Holmwood*. They later told the *Holmwood* captives that the raiders had been lying in wait for the steamer in order to replenish its supply of fresh meat. This implied that the raiders had known exactly when and where *Holmwood* would be sailing. The war memoirs of *Komet's* and *Orion*'s commanders made no reference to knowing the intended movements of *Holmwood*, but rumours and speculation among the captives were rife. Eyssen's diary recorded that his prize crew had captured twenty-three navigation charts, lighthouse identifications, code books, radio sets, cameras and instructions on wartime procedures, particularly on radio transmissions. He recorded in particular the capture of the *Bentley Complete Phrase Code* and found that he would be able to de-code relatively low security radio telegrams. The Bentley code was an American system that had been in use since the First World War and enabled commercial organisations, shipping companies and their agents to communicate in code, albeit a code known to everybody with access to the widely available Bentley code book. As well as giving a low level of security, it was also used at a time when the cost of radio telegrams was calculated by the number of words in the message. By using codes for standard messages, shipping companies could save on their telegram costs. It is known that the British Phosphate Commissioners who operated the phosphate trade at Nauru, the raiders' destination, used the Bentley code. It seems unlikely that the raiders already had a copy of the Bentley code: Eyssen would not have bothered to boast about capturing it. The other method of encoding messages in common use was Playfair, a relatively simple cypher method which only needed a key phrase, not a book of codes. Again, it was known to be in use in both New Zealand and Australia and, although easy to use, it was difficult to decypher unless the message was long or the key phrase was not changed for a long period of time. It was therefore used for relatively short time span operational messages where, if the message was eventually decrypted, the need for secrecy had elapsed.

Eyssen was particularly pleased at having captured the British Admiralty's instructions to merchant shipping on wartime procedures, although he commented that most of it would probably be known to his intelligence service back in Berlin. He recorded that allied ships were required to sail a zigzag course unless visibility was less than two miles. Every ship was also required to report suspicious vessels and there were detailed instructions on revocation of raider warning messages. It was well known that after ships had transmitted warning messages, German raiders would transmit a false message pretending to revoke or cancel the warning. Eyssen learnt that a special signal had to be coded in merchant navy code and transmitted to prove that it was a genuine revocation of a warning. Eyssen even recorded that his radio officers successfully decoded copies of Bentley coded radio messages found on *Holmwood*, but failed to decode some other messages; whether these were in merchant navy code or Playfair is not known. He also said that they had captured a previously unknown schedule of transmission times for merchant shipping broadcasts. This was most likely to have been the allied BAMS system of updating all shipping on weather and current events and threats in different operational areas.

Eyssen's claim in his memoirs that he captured intelligence material from *Holmwood* is at variance with the evidence given by Captain Miller and Chief Officer Campbell at the 1941 inquiry. Miller said, and Campbell agreed, that the confidential material had been put in a bag weighted with a large spanner and dropped over the side. Eyssen's claim is the more credible: although he was a consummate boaster in his memoirs, the level of detail he used to describe the material and his evident delight at having it, appear genuine. The 1941 inquiry established that the *Holmwood*'s survivors had colluded when compiling their personal diaries of events and it is possible, but not proven, that none or not all the confidential papers had been disposed of. The most charitable explanation is that Campbell only dumped the merchant navy codebooks.

The prisoners were introduced to their new home. Eyssen had a long talk with Captain Miller who, Eyssen recorded, made a very favourable impression on him. Miller was told that he would be responsible for the conduct and tidiness of the prisoners and that no personal possessions would be permanently confiscated. Eyssen also told Miller that everybody would be accommodated in bunks, would receive the same food as the crew and that his officers would vacate their cabins to ensure that the women and children had privacy. He even said that they would have deck chairs to sit in when they were allowed on deck. Evidence given by survivors in 1941 confirmed that Eyssen had been true to his word.

In his wartime memoirs, *Orion*'s Captain Kurt Weyher said that the captured sheep caused quite a stir: after the initial diversion of sheep-back racing by *Orion's* crew around her decks, he said that it took two days to slaughter and butcher the sheep. After eight months at sea the crew were delighted to have the fresh mutton, but in the following days the meat became somewhat monotonous and finally became abhorrent. This is in contrast to some of the subsequent captives' reports which said that the meagre rations that they had to endure were the same that the crew's.

Chapter 4

Rangitane's last day

Monday 25 and Tuesday 26 November on *Rangitane* passed without incident. Life was typical of a passenger liner - plenty of deck games and activities for the passengers to explore. The CORB escorts had enjoyed an unexpected holiday in New Zealand while waiting to join a ship for the return journey to England. In November it was early summer but the weather was still chilly. They had been entertained by officials and families in and around Wellington - even having morning tea and cakes in Government House with the Prime Minister. On a trip along the coast it was pure coincidence that they saw their beloved *Batory* sailing away in her newly painted convoy livery, laden with troops going to war and closely shadowed by HMNZS *Achilles*. *Batory* was to sail to Melbourne to make up a convoy with the troopships SS *Strathmore* and SS *Stratheden*, all of whom would eventually arrive safely in Egypt.

The CORB escorts had visited local tourist sights and travelled to a traditional Maori village, buying mementoes which they later used to decorate their cabins on *Rangitane*, vying with each other as to who could have the best display. But this was no holiday cruise: life had a darker side because of the ever-present dangers of war. On each of the first two days the passengers and crew carried out lifeboat drills, little knowing that soon they would be putting the practice into real action. For the CORB escorts the boat drills were completely different from those on *Batory*. This time they only had themselves and their own lifebelts to tie up; on *Batory* they had hundreds of over-excited children to worry about. The lifeboat drills instructed the passengers on the warning they would receive to abandon ship and the location of their allocated lifeboats. Everybody, crew and passengers alike had prepared a 'panic-bag' containing essentials in the event of emergency evacuation. The officers on the bridge were blissfully unaware that three German raiders were already converging on their course. On the night of Tuesday 26 November, 1940, Captain Upton handed control of his *Tane* over to Henry Williams, his Second Officer, before retiring to his bunk. Lookouts had been posted, as usual, in the crow's nest, on the forecastle head, one on each of the bridge wings, two on the top of the dummy funnel and two gunners next to the aft gun.

At 3.35 on the morning of Wednesday 27 November the lookout in the crow's nest rang his bell to report a strange ship with no lights crossing *Rangitane*'s bows from starboard to port about half a mile away; almost immediately one of the gun crew reported another ship on the port beam. Such an occurrence was completely out of the ordinary and Williams called Captain Upton who was asleep in his cabin. Upton thought that it might be a ship bound to or from Antarctica but immediately went to the bridge with his uniform over his pyjamas. Williams had also rung the engine room to warn them of imminent manoeuvring and the engineering watch officer rang the breakdown bell to call the engine room crew from their bunks to their stations. When Upton had gained his night-eyes he saw three ships: he knew that there were no Allied armed merchant ships due in the region. He suspected that they were German raiders who had until then been working laying mines and harassing shipping off the New Zealand coast. Upton told First Officer Hopkins to get all hands on deck and to man the *Rangitane* gun. He told Hopkins that if the order was given, the gun layer should aim for the midships section of the nearest raider. Upton then mused that the gun with its allocation of only forty shells would only last three to four minutes. He decided not to return fire if they were attacked, deciding that *Rangitane* could withstand a certain amount of gun damage, but certainly not a torpedo. He also decided not to give the emergency signal to the passengers because the evacuation meeting point was the public room on the lifeboat deck, immediately below the radio room which would be a prime target for the raiders' gunners.

One of the raiders signalled by lamp in Morse code for *Rangitane* to stop and not to use the radio, but Upton and his officers were too busy to read the message. Following Admiralty standing orders, Captain Upton ordered the QQQQ radio signal to be sent - the standard armed merchant ship raider message. As soon as the Radio Officer started sending the message the raiders immediately tried to jam the transmission, switched on searchlights and started shelling *Rangitane.* The radio officer tried to send the QQQQ message again. At only half a mile distance *Rangitane* didn't stand a chance: one of the first shells hit the radio mast before the message had been sent. Upton knew that it was imperative that the authorities should be told that he was under attack, so the emergency radio transmitter was brought into action while valves in the main radio were replaced. It was later learned that one of the raiders had difficulty finding a range because the searchlight was reflected by the fine drizzle. That same raider, which had been dogged by persistent mechanical problems, found that its steering engine had jammed and it was only able to sail directly towards *Rangitane.* Upton rang down to the engine room for maximum power and ordered the ship to starboard to present the stern to the raider that he thought posed the greatest danger. In the engine room the crew were still unaware of the seriousness of what was happening outside and were surprised at the urgent demands being placed on the engines. In his personal account, Captain Upton said that *Rangitane* decided that she did not like the Germans because she suddenly turned towards another of the raiders and ironically proceeded at seventeen knots on a collision course, a speed never previously achieved, even on trials. Upton said that she obviously thought better of it and started circling again. The Quartermaster at the wheel then reported that *Rangitane* was not answering her helm: her steering mechanism had obviously been damaged and *Rangitane* was out of control.

Norman Hallett, the radio officer, finally confirmed that New Zealand radio stations had received and were re-transmitting the raider attack message and Captain Upton ordered his ship to be stopped, the ensign to be lowered and the Radio Officer to stop transmitting. He was aware that there was already extensive damage and that there were fires on decks A to E and that he had lost steering capability. He then signalled the raiders that there were women on board and that he was stopping. There followed a frantic attempt to collect and destroy any secret or incriminating documents and to collect personal items and warm clothes before abandoning ship. But the shelling continued and Upton later recorded that this really annoyed him. He said that he wanted to take a shot at the raiders, ordered full speed again and tried to telephone the gunners to open fire, only to find that the telephone on the gun platform had been destroyed. The shelling suddenly stopped and Upton ordered that *Rangitane* had to be abandoned.

Third Electrician Jack Almond later recounted how vital parts of *Rangitane*'s engines were destroyed with sledgehammers to ensure that the Germans didn't try to take the ship as a war prize. Captain Upton's actions were praised by the 1941 official inquiry into the whole episode. The only minor criticism was that it transpired that *Rangitane's* gun had been under a protective cover: had Captain Upton been in a position to retaliate, he would have been delayed while the gun was uncovered.

The shelling started at 3.47 a.m. and ended at 3.59 a.m. From just a few minutes' shelling there were dead and injured scattered throughout the decks. Five passengers, all CORB evacuee escorts, and five crewmen died in a short space of time, either from direct injury or from drowning. In the following days and weeks another three passengers and three crew members died on the raiders from their injuries, sixteen in total.

One of the CORB escorts killed was forty-four year old Doris Beeston from Grange, Australia. She had won a scholarship to a social welfare course in London where she was studying on the outbreak of war. She offered to escort the evacuees to Australia on condition that she could return to London and continue her studies. Another CORB escort to die was twenty-seven year old James Dixon from Kelburn, Wellington. He was quite a well known sportsman and had gone to England to work for the Ministry of Labour, creating work opportunities for children from deprived areas. He volunteered as a CORB escort and had travelled from Australia to New Zealand to see his family before returning to England on *Rangitane.* Elsie Davies, a twenty-nine year old Baptist clergyman's wife from north London was killed. She was reported to have a university degree and had always been laughing and joking with her evacuees on *Batory.* She was particularly remembered for her use of a well known slogan at the time: 'Careless talk costs lives' she would say sternly if she heard her children talking after lights-out. Andrew Tocher, a fifty-seven year old retired bank manager from Scotland was killed; he had been an elder of the Church of Scotland. One of the crew to die was Francis Pithers from Gillingham in Kent; at just sixteen years old he was a steward's boy on *Rangitane.*

It is worth considering how devastating a high explosive shell blast can be in a confined space. The shells were from a 15 cm (5.9-inch) gun identical to those on the German raider *Kormoran* which was to engage and sink HMAS *Sydney* in late 1941. The 2010 inquiry into the loss of the *Sydney* took evidence from the Australian government's DSTO department who said that each shell weighed 45.3 kg and was designed to splinter on impact generating a minimum of 200,000 individual steel fragments and thousands of secondary fragments. The effect of a single shell in *Rangitane*'s relatively weak upper decks would have been horrific: as well as the searingly hot steel shrapnel, there would have been large timber splinters flying around.

The port deck containing the CORB escorts' cabins bore the brunt of the attack. The escorts were all volunteers who had offered their services as their contribution to the war effort. When they had been sailing from Liverpool to Australia on *Batory* with their 477 evacuees, it had been impressed upon them to keep their cabin doors fixed open at all times to prevent them becoming jammed shut if the ship came under attack. They had also been told that they and their children must only go on deck if expressly told to do so by somebody in authority. When the first shells hit *Rangitane*, the cabins disintegrated but the escorts dutifully stayed in the smoke and dust. The elegant stairway from the dining-room, the centrepiece signifying the elegant age of ocean cruising, had been completely demolished. In addition to those killed outright, many of the others sustained injury. One, Miss Phyllis Matthews, a nursing home nurse from Devon had lost an arm; most of the others had wounds of varying degrees. One woman, Florence Mundie, a nursing Sister in inside cabin 61 on C deck had horrific facial injuries and had most of her clothes burnt off. Had it not been for an engineer and the chief officer who quickly got her into a boiler suit and into a boat, she would have perished on *Rangitane*. Fortunately Florence was to survive well into her eighties despite her horrific injuries. Una Scott, in cabin C62 across the corridor but nearer the port side from Florence, was not so lucky - she was killed instantly. The CORB dentist, Eileen Sutcliffe-Hey and known to everybody as 'SH' had a miraculous escape: her cabin on C deck collapsed and she fell one complete deck into the first class dining room. Although injured and dazed she was quickly rescued.

The injured on *Rangitane* were taken to the passenger lounge where they were given first-aid. Stewards and cooks became comforters and the fit helped the injured. Frank Ellison, a young steward from Lancashire recalls helping an injured young woman to a lifeboat. Elizabeth Plumb, a fifty-nine year old stewardess in the first class accommodation who had joined

Rangitane in 1938 tended many of the wounded until they reached a raider. Although wounded herself, she refused treatment until the others had been attended to. It was not until she fainted from loss of blood did the German doctors realise the seriousness of her wounds from shrapnel and it was mid-day when they operated on her. Her husband had been killed 20 years previously in an accident and she had been left to bring up four children by herself. She was later awarded the British Empire Medal, as were ship's cook William Francis and deck mechanic John Walker who were commended for their bravery in rescuing survivors.

Just as dawn was breaking, motor launches containing prize crews were despatched from the raiders. It is clear that there was a race between the prize crews to get to *Rangitane* first. *Orion's* captain noted in his diary his frustration that his prize crew had been delayed by a rope fouling the launch's propeller. The German sailors ordered the immediate evacuation of *Rangitane*: they were clearly aware that the raider warning message had been successfully transmitted and wanted to leave the area as quickly as possible. The crew and passengers grabbed their panic-bags and warm clothes and took to the lifeboats, some of which had already been damaged by earlier shellfire. Two officers clutched sextants, radio officer James Ward cradled his prized typewriter while others managed to conceal their ships' chronometers and personal cameras. Although many of these items were later confiscated, it is surprising that everything was eventually returned to their rightful owners. Third Engineer John Colwell unscrewed the engine room clock, put it in his panic bag and then forgot to take it with him to the lifeboat while Geoffrey Barley made sure that he had his baby panda lucky mascot in his bag. The mascot obviously worked for Barley - he survived the ordeal and went on to become a captain after the war. Father Ball later recounted how he must have been totally confused when he went back into his cabin to recover only his travelling clock, discarding other considerably more useful items.

Young German seamen supervised the evacuation, the first time that any passengers or crew had come literally face to face with their enemy. Nobody experienced any form of hostility or brutality: the Germans were doing their job in a professional and humane manner, something which would become even more apparent in the following days. The behaviour and attitude of the passengers and crew was exemplary, each waiting their turn to board lifeboats without panic or outward anguish. Passengers were shepherded by the crew in a most professional manner and Captain Upton later recorded how proud he was to have been in command of such a magnificent party of people. One survivor described the scene as being like a church parade with people moving slowly and talking only in whispers. In reality it is likely that pure shock at the dramatic change of circumstance had stunned everybody into private thought and personal anguish. The passengers had been allocated to lifeboat stations in alphabetical order. Margaret Osborne, one of the CORB escorts said afterwards that she was distraught when she realised that while she would be in lifeboat four, while Ella Clothier, her cabin-mate and close friend, would be on lifeboat ten. As it turned out, both lifeboats were directed to the same raider. It was unfortunate that, even in the hour of danger to all, the two first class passengers felt that their position in society should command priority in the lifeboats.

The last three people to leave *Rangitane* were Captain Upton, the Chief Engineer and the Chief Officer. It was poignant that Second Engineer Edgar and Fourth Engineer Hodgeson had been asked to go back to the engine room and shut down the generators: it was as if Captain Upton wanted the lights turned out and doors closed before leaving his *Tane* for the last time.

There was quite a deep swell in the sea and the survivors were eager to get their lifeboats away from *Rangitane* in case she suddenly sank. Some of the lifeboats were powered by a patent hand-cranked propeller: no skill was required to operate hand levers and anybody could propel the boats. Tom Newland, one of the Fleet Air Arm recruits, was on lifeboat number ten which was launched successfully but a rope had fouled the propeller. He spent many cold minutes diving underwater, trying to remove the rope. One of the crew then tried but gave up when a raider launch took them in tow. Father Ball, a CORB escort, wrote that on his lifeboat they found rum and cigarettes. After helping themselves they threw the majority of the cigarettes overboard so they wouldn't fall into the hands of the Germans, an action they bitterly regretted a few weeks later when good tobacco was in short supply. Father Ball also said that he was ignominiously sea-sick on the short journey to the raider.

Rangitane's crew and passengers being transferred to the raiders

Looking back at *Rangitane,* she was clearly badly ablaze, listing slightly and it is was obvious that she would not survive the attack. Lifeboat number eight still hung on its davits, its side shattered by the shelling. The raiders' launches looked menacing because each had a manned machinegun amidships; worries of being killed in the lifeboats were compounded when some of the gunners pointed the guns menacingly, but in the noise and confusion it was the only way that the captors could persuade each lifeboat to move towards a specified raider. The *Manchester Guardian* newspaper dramatically reported this as 'Women Shot in Lifeboats.' Lifeboat number eleven was full and carried many of the RNZAF men and also Florence Mundie who had the facial injuries. None of them realised that the lifeboat had been holed by shrapnel and it started taking on water. The men baled her out but could not stem the flow and reluctantly most of the able-bodied decided to swim for it. The lifeboat was nearly swamped and Florence Mundie tried to get out but was pulled back by young Reg Moore, a smoking room steward who struggled to keep her head above water. Finally a launch from *Komet* arrived and its crew dragged the survivors aboard. Florence found two other serious casualties on the launch - brothers Fred and Sam Strickfuss who worked in the *Rangitane* engine room with their father. The *Komet* launch then gave tow to another lifeboat clearly in difficulties. Friends helping Miss Matthews in her lifeboat feared for her life: her arm was completely shattered and she was losing blood quickly. Thanks to the work of the German doctors, Miss Matthews' life was saved, but she lost her arm.

Some damaged lifeboats only just made it

Captain Upton together with his Chief Engineer and Chief Officer were towed towards *Komet* while the majority of the engineering officers were sent to *Kulmerland.* Able Seaman Ron Smith was in charge of a lifeboat that was directed to *Orion*, while the Second Officer Williams was in control of another boat heading for *Kulmerland.* Those survivors who were injured or carrying bulky personal items found it difficult to climb aboard the raiders from lifeboats rising and falling in the swell. Some of the women suffered rough handling to get them on board quickly but accepted that

The last moments of RMS Rangitane

it was a better alternative than being abandoned to the sea. Some of the *Rangitane* crew were clearly the worse for drink: Geoffrey Barley recorded that many crew had mysteriously acquired bottles of whisky, while Captain Eyssen wrote in his diary that several people were fortified with alcohol. Captain Weyher of *Orion* claimed that he plied some of the air force men with alcohol to loosen their tongues and learn about the New Zealand air defences. Barley also commented that many of the survivors wore their habitual smile while others looked just as miserable as they did normally.

Those who had died in the lifeboats were covered and the lifeboats scuttled. *Kulmerland* hoisted two lifeboats onto its deck - Eyssen wrote in his diary 'Pschunder' (*Kulmerland*'s captain) 'has started collecting boats!' Had *Rangitane* been captured undamaged she would have been a valuable asset to the Germans. One of *Kulmerland*'s officers later confessed his disappointment at not being able to take a prize crew and sail *Rangitane* and her 14,000 tons of cargo back to Germany. The damage was too great; nearly three hours after the first attack, fires had started in the cargo holds. After completing their search, the prize crew opened the sea cocks and *Rangitane* started to list slightly to port. But the Germans were aware that the raider warning may have been received and it would only take a few hours before planes would reach the scene. They were anxious to leave quickly and to destroy all evidence of their presence. *Rangitane* was despatched by a single torpedo from *Komet*, listing quickly to port and finally disappearing under the waves at 6.30 a.m. to settle at 4,300 fathoms at 36° 58' S, 175° 22' W.

Thankfully, none of the *Rangitane* survivors saw her sink; they had all been taken below decks and were busy assessing the surroundings that were to be their home for the foreseeable future. Those taken to *Komet* were surprised to find twenty-nine New Zealanders, including women and children, from the *Holmwood* already in residence. Those taken to *Orion* found over sixty sailors from the *Ringwood* and *Turakina* sunk in the previous months.

The raider warning messages had certainly been received by the authorities in New Zealand and caused an immediate alert. All shipping was warned to stay at least 200 miles away from *Rangitane*'s reported position. HMNZS *Achilles*, New Zealand's most famous warship and a key player in the battle of the River Plate, was provisioning in Lyttelton. She was a *Leander* class light cruiser with a maximum speed of thirty-two knots. Many of her crew were due to go on long leave a few days later but the chance of catching some German raiders made up for the disappointment of having their leave cancelled. *Achilles* cleared harbour just after 8 a.m. and made twenty-five knots northwards. Not to be outdone, MV *Puriri* had her engines re-assembled specially to join the search, leaving Auckland at 7 p.m. The flying boats *Aotearoa* and *Awarua* joined in, as did the MV *Monowai.* The first on the scene was the *Aotearoa* at about 2.30 p.m., only to find deck furniture and the debris of the shelling floating in a huge expanse of oil. There was no sign of *Rangitane*, her survivors, or her aggressors. *Achilles* arrived at dawn on the next day to see an eighteen square mile oil slick dotted with butter boxes and red and white lifebelts. Despite extended searches by aircraft, they did not see the raiders.

However, the raiders saw one search aircraft momentarily at about 6 p.m. and were amazed that they had not been spotted. It was the first major alert on the raiders and many of the prisoners had mixed feelings - their lives would have been at risk for the second time that day if the aircraft attacked. As it turned out, the aircraft turned away, much to the disgust of Judge Stuart and his wife, the first class passengers. Stuart was so incensed at what he saw as a scandal that he later reported the incident to the security services and said that whoever was responsible for not taking action on the sighting 'should be placed under control for the duration of the war.'

Chapter 5

The German raiders

So started the survivors' first day as prisoners-of-war. What was immediately obvious was that each ship had been designed to accommodate prisoners. The cargo holds on *Komet* and *Orion* had been turned into barrack-type rooms, some with bunks lining the walls and bulkheads. There was a plentiful supply of hammocks, new mugs and plates - many still showing signs of their original packaging and quite evidently supplied in Japan. But other things were clearly in short supply - fresh water for washing and, more seriously, nutritious food. Prison life was also different on the three ships, possibly a reflection of the attitude of the captains and their crew.

The captain of *Komet* was Robert Eyssen, the most senior of the three captains. He assumed overall command of the raiders, dubbing them his Far Eastern Squadron. There were to be several exchanges and disagreements over tactics and long term strategy, particularly with Kurt Weyher, *Orion's* captain. Eyssen was an experienced officer in his fifties, having joined the *Kaiserliche Marine* in 1911. As already described, *Komet* was originally the freighter *Ems*, built in 1936 and displacing 3,287 tons. *Komet* had been converted to a raider in early 1940 and carried six six-inch guns, anti-aircraft guns and six torpedo tubes. She was the smallest of all of the auxiliary cruisers. The main feature of German raiders was that they hid their armament within false superstructure that could be dropped within seconds.

Robert Eyssen

Even at close range the raiders looked like any innocent merchant ship, the effect being enhanced by displaying the names and flags of officially neutral countries - particularly Japan. *Komet* had the ability to change her profile: wooden frames could quickly be erected from the well-decks to give the impression of being a flush-deck freighter. She also had on board a relatively old design Arado sea-plane called *Sparrow* which, on the occasional days that it was working, gave the raider long range reconnaissance capability. Similarly, *Komet* had a light minelayer speedboat called *Meteorit* which was to prove very unreliable.

KMS Komet

Komet and her 270 crew left Germany at the beginning of July 1940 and sailed the dangerous arctic route and around Siberia with the help of the Russians' marine pilots and icebreakers. This was an amazing achievement in itself but would have ended in disaster had it not been for the Russian assistance. Their help had been at a price - 950,000 Reichsmark was the reported payment to them. From there she sailed down to the Japanese island of Lamotrek in the Caroline Islands and met *Orion* and *Kulmerland* in mid-October. After a conference on strategy, the three captains decided to work together, concentrating on the New Zealand to Panama passage, the route taken by most of the Allied merchant ships. They decided on Japanese disguises - *Komet* and *Kulmerland* had the names *Manyo Maru* and *Tokio Maru* painted on their hulls. By the time they sank *Holmwood* and *Rangitane*, *Komet* had already been at sea for 140 days and Eyssen admitted in his war diaries that he had become depressed and frustrated at not having encountered the enemy. In his diary he made a very cryptic remark: he wrote that *Rangitane* by itself would make up a substantial part of his quota. It can only be assumed that he had been given a quota or target to sink by German naval command. *Komet's* overall war record was not to be very impressive and Eyssen continued to be troubled by the lack of success. Survivors held prisoner on *Komet* generally thought of him as a gentleman, if somewhat pompous.

Kurt Weyher, also a career naval officer, was the commander of *Orion* and had seen considerably more action than Eyssen. His ship was larger at 7,021 tons and had been built in 1930 as the freighter *Kurmark* of the Hamburg-Amerika Line, commonly known at the Hapag line. She was converted into a raider at the beginning of 1940 with the same armament as *Komet*. But *Orion* had one major problem - her engines had been salvaged from Hapag's passenger liner *New York* and they became a constant source of aggravation during *Orion's* sixteen month tour of duty. Weyher was thirty-nine years old when he took command of *Orion*, leaving Germany at the beginning of April 1940 and proving over the summer months that he was a formidable commander. He disguised his ship as Dutch, Russian, Greek and Japanese and succeeded in sinking six ships and laying mines that were to claim another six. By the time *Orion* met up with *Komet* and *Kulmerland* in October at Lamotrek, Weyher was already a seasoned commander. It must have been frustrating for him to operate in the company of Eyssen, a superior officer, with whom he clearly had difficulties, and not to have had any enemy action between mid-October and the time they found the *Holmwood*

Kurt Weyher

and *Rangitane.* The impression gained is that Eyssen's age and rank made him more tolerant and amenable to the prisoners' needs whereas the humourous but volatile Weyher was still a rising star and may have felt the need to impose his authority on his ship and his prisoners. There is evidence that when Weyher disagreed with Eyssen, he made sure that German naval command was aware of the differences.

KMS Orion

There is also evidence that Eyssen and Weyher may have been acquainted for a very long time: they are both listed as being members of the *Löwenfeld* Third Marine Brigade, an unofficial troop created by disaffected naval officers after Germany's capitulation in 1918. It is quite possible that they were horrified at how the *Kaiserliche Marine* had degenerated into the naval mutiny in the final months of the war when ships' engine stokers refused to let the German fleet sail for what they thought would be a suicidal battle against the British Grand Fleet. Based in Kiel, the brigade was one of the first of many reactionary *Freikorps* who combined in the 1920 *Kapp Putsch* revolution, intent on overthrowing the newly formed Weimar Republic and countering the rapid expansion of communism in Germany. The right-wing putsch failed but it incubated the rise of an even more reactionary force ten years later.

Although *Orion* was temporarily named *Maebasi Maru*, that name was never shown on her: she was painted a sinister black and was to become known by the prisoners as the *'Black Raider.'* *Orion* is sometimes referred to as *Narvik*. This is incorrect: *Orion's* sister ship *Widder*, which was also a successful surface raider, often adopted the disguise of the Norwegian vessel *Narvik*.

The supply ship *Kulmerland* was another ex-Hapag vessel. Built in 1928, she had been a 7,363 ton passenger and cargo ship operating between Hamburg and New York. On the outbreak of war she was requisitioned by the German navy to keep surface raiders provisioned at sea. Captain Wilhelm Pschunder had been her master since she was launched. He was in his sixties and described as short, sandy-haired and kindly. He was not a navy man: he had clearly been more comfortable entertaining his fare-paying guests at the captain's table and was most unsuited for the life of a disciplinarian under the Nazi regime. Others described him as being as genial as was possible under the circumstances of war, and were particularly moved by the apparently genuine emotion he displayed when his prisoners finally left his ship. Most of Pschunder's crew were older merchant seamen, not *Kriegsmarine* sailors. *Kulmerland* was unarmed, painted white to display a degree of neutrality and was equipped with good medical facilities, including an operating theatre and x-ray equipment, all of which were to be used extensively over the few weeks after the sinking of *Rangitane*.

Raider supply ship Kulmerland

The survivors had been distributed randomly between the three ships. Captain Upton and his senior officers were on *Komet*, together with twelve RNZAF men and most of the women prisoners. Most of the engineering and radio officers were on *Kulmerland*, and *Orion* had many of the seamen, stewards and Polish stewardesses from *Batory*. Everybody was forced below decks and the Germans' first objective was to get away from *Rangitane's* last reported position. The first day allowed the prisoners to take stock of their predicament. While some of the passengers and crew had sufficient time to grab their panic bags and a few suitable clothes, the CORB escorts, whose cabins had taken the brunt of the initial attack, were far from suitably dressed and had to use some ingenuity to improvise clothes and footwear. Other people found that they had forgotten or mislaid spectacles or false teeth. Few had such basic necessities as tooth brushes and combs. Personal hygiene was not helped by the lack of fresh water for washing: each of the women was given a small bar of soap which, they were told, had to last one month. Little did they realise that the lack of washing water would mean that the soap would last more than a month. While these privations were bad enough, the biggest problem was the food. A daily diet of thin soup, glutinous rice or macaroni, ersatz coffee and stale black bread did nothing for morale. In hindsight, the lack of nutritious food seems strange bearing in mind that so many sheep had been captured from *Holmwood* only two days earlier. The fact that everybody was in the same predicament was a source of wry amusement: the evening before *Rangitane* was sunk, the first class steward had been obsequiously serving dinner to Judge and Mrs Stuart, who had already proved their contempt of people not of their class. Now, Judge Stuart had to share a meagre bowl of rice with that same steward, spooning it with bamboo sticks picked off the deck, while Mrs Stuart was frequently cut down to size, mainly by the Polish stewardesses from *Batory*. As one of the passengers noted, adversity is a great equaliser. *Orion's* Captain Weyher noted that his most difficult prisoners were the Polish stewardesses: initially they bluntly refused any form of co-operation, expecting to be waited upon and scorning the normal daily routine.

During the afternoon of the first day, Wednesday 27 November, the two Strickfuss brothers on *Komet* died from their injuries. Fred Strickfuss was twenty and Stanley Strickfuss was twenty-seven. They were both Greasers in the engine-room where their father, Sam, also worked as a Donkeyman. Their father had witnessed his sons' injuries and helped them into their lifeboat. He then went to his assigned lifeboat and, as fate had it, was directed to a different raider. At about 6 p.m. *Komet* stopped and the Strickfuss boys' bodies, draped in a home-made Union Jack, were escorted by a German NCO and six of *Komet's* crew, all in dress uniforms. Captain Upton and First Officer Ernest Hopkins were allowed to be present to witness what Captain Eyssen called a 'short but solemn seaman's funeral.'

The first days were very different on the three ships. On *Orion*, Captain Weyher's crew formally interviewed their new captives individually. They were intent on finding out as much as possible about other ships in New Zealand, their ports of call and the route to be taken by *Rangitane*. In his memoirs, Weyher said that useful documents had been found on *Rangitane* concerning the defensive measures taken by Australia and New Zealand to counter the threat of the raiders. He even claimed to have found information on the swept channel out of Auckland. Although most valuables and personal possessions were taken away, everybody received receipts. It was reported that secret microphones had been installed in the areas holding the prisoners and that conversations were being recorded. Rumour obviously led to paranoia: there was some concern among some of the *Orion* prisoners that the Polish men from *Batory* were becoming too familiar with their captors, particularly those who spoke and shared confidences in German. All sorts of fifth columnist rumours started and later became sensationalised by the Australian press. When referring to the two Polish seamen who were alleged to have been deserters, one press report said that they had deliberately not blacked-out the porthole of their cabin on *Rangitane*. They were alleged to have been awake, fully dressed with their bags packed as if they were expecting the attack and had given a Nazi salute and welcomed the German prize crew as friends, speaking in fluent German.

The first days on the two other ships were more relaxed: the captives were allowed to keep their personal possessions and there was little attempt at interrogation, but everybody began to realise that the lack of food would be their biggest problem. As usually happens at such times, the more comic of the captives resorted to song, composing a tribute to the food to the tune of 'The Quartermaster's Stores':

There was rice, rice, rice full of lice,
In the stores, the German raider's stores;
There was bread, bread, like lumps of lead,
In the stores, the German raider's stores;
My eyes are dim, I cannot see,
I left my specs on the Rangitane,
I left my specs on the Rangitane!

The most senior ranking British seaman on *Orion* was the Purser, Edward Maugham and he initially assumed the role as the prisoners' commander and spokesman. Father Ball recalled that Maugham 'did not have the qualities required and there was an evident unwillingness to acknowledge his authority.' Maugham was replaced by somebody whom Father Ball described as a most unlikely candidate but soon proved his capability. Although Father Ball did not name the person he said that there was an allegation that he was a naval rating on his way back to England as a passenger to face a court-martial. It is possible that this person could have been B. G. Fitzsimons, one of the few passengers unaffiliated to any group or organization.

Most of the survivors knew that there had been injuries and fatalities during the engagement. One of the CORB escorts wrote later how surprised she was at the medical facilities that were available on all three raiders and how dedicated the German medical crew were. In fact, those CORB escorts who were nurses started a shift system to provide continuous care for the injured. But not everybody survived the care. Elinor Herbert-Jones was a twenty-one year old CORB escort who received serious back and chest wounds. She was the youngest escort on *Batory* and had evidently stolen a few hearts during the journey to Australia. But she was totally committed to her job, saying 'Love me, love my evacuees.' Seriously injured, she had been taken to *Orion* and underwent intensive care but died on the following day. Another CORB escort, Sister Rosalie Golding was asked by the Germans to lay out Elinor's body. While Elinor's friends and colleagues were distraught, they were amazed when they found that there was to be a formal burial at sea. Just as daylight was fading and Captain Weyher thought it safe to stop, the survivors were led onto the deck to find a parade of about 150 *Orion's* crew, all smartly presented in their white uniforms, their black cap bands fluttering in the evening breeze. In front of them were the officers, immaculate in dress uniform and gloves.

The female prisoners were offered chairs while the men stood to the side. Rosalie Golding recorded later that they resolutely refused to sit: she wrote 'We women felt we were British and we would stand.' Looking up, the prisoners contemplated an anachronism: the German swastika flying at half-mast. Resting on the side rail was Elinor's bier, lying on a Union Jack and draped with a Red Ensign. The poignancy of the occasion was clearly not lost on anybody. Captain Weyher approached the funeral party, saluted the prisoners and presented a long and passionate oration in German, obviously for the benefit of his own crew. One observer associated his style of presentation to that of Hitler. It had evidently been a very carefully prepared speech because an English translation was later circulated to the prisoners:

> Comrades of the German Navy! People of other nations! Every people and every nation has the right, in its fight for

freedom, to call upon all men capable of bearing arms, sons of the people, to demand the highest sacrifices that have to be made for the freedom of their people. We Germans have been forced into this war against our will. In this war the nation can demand such sacrifices, even the life of its manhood under arms.

It is not unusual for us, as soldiers, to see a soldier, a man, fall before the enemy, giving his life's blood for his country. For the first time on this ship, however, we do not see a man, but a woman, fall in action.

It is not the will of the German people or of the German Government to wage a war against women or children, or to extend the war abnormally; but the British Government has drawn women and children into the sphere of war. The British people have wanted it so, and we Germans, who must necessarily defend our country, our freedom, our women and our children's future, cannot recoil from any sacrifice, either for us or for others. That is the inexorable law of this war which has been forced on us.

Nevertheless it is extremely sad and moving for us, as soldiers and sailors, to have been placed in the position of having to bury a woman fallen in action on the high sea. I believe, my German comrades, that not one of us would wish our women and children to be exposed to the dangers and hard laws of the war at sea, no matter for what reason. If another country, however, sees fit to do so, it is not our task to pass judgement over that matter here, in view of the death and sacrifice of another nation's woman. Miss Herbert Jones took upon herself the task of accompanying children, through the dangers of war at sea, from England to New Zealand, a measure which it is not for us to pass judgement on here, as has already been stated. For her this meant consciously taking the dangers and sacrifices upon herself which war at sea brings with it.

I believe that all sailors on board, whether friend or foe, realise that the laws of the sea are hard in themselves, and that war at sea, our element, is inexorable and demands great sacrifices.

In sharp contrast, there followed a quiet committal service from the Reverend Father Ball, who had accompanied the children on *Batory*. He wrote out the service from memory and had to submit it to Captain Weyher for approval. Captain Weyher then said 'We shall now place the deceased in the hands of our element, the eternal sea, on which we shall continue to sail freely; that same sea has now become the fate of this woman.' Elinor's body was then piped over the side, committed to the deep. The ship's loudspeaker broadcast a traditional German march 'Ich hatt einen Kameraden' (I had a comrade.) The ship's company was dismissed with a 'Heil Hitler' salute from Captain Weyher.

The fact that Weyher had held a funeral ceremony is typical of the overall attitude of the Germans towards their prisoners. With only one dissention, the general opinion was that the captors showed as much respect and courtesy as was possible under the circumstances of war. The *Rangitane* officers reported that the German crew would always salute and remove their cap when they entered the prisoners' rooms and the women captives said that their captors would always remove their caps and bow respectfully. There were many reports of good humour and banter and many instances of personal good deeds carried out by crewmen. Overall, the Germans treated the survivors as unwanted guests and not as prisoners. There was only one report of ill-treatment which was roundly rejected by the official inquiry into the sinking of *Rangitane* held in 1941: Judge Stuart, who did little to endear himself to either the Germans or his fellow prisoners, alleged that they were treated shockingly unless they made concessions to their captors. In a surprisingly blunt dismissal, particularly in view of Stuart's position as a judge, the inquiry concluded '... the account generally given of Mr. Stuart by his fellow-captives conveys an unfavourable impression as to his accuracy and reliability.' Mrs. Stuart made great play of the fact that she was a niece of Dr.

Leander Starr Jameson, the famous colonialist and politician who in 1904 became the tenth Prime Minister of Cape Colony in South Africa. Mrs. Stuart was in fact an extremely well educated and prominent lady. She was a graduate of Oxford University and had degrees from the Sorbonne in Paris and an unnamed German university. In 1937 she was a candidate for the Senate in Cape Province, South Africa, losing the election by only three votes. Had she been elected, she claimed she would have been the only woman senator in the British Empire.

Judge William and Mrs. Starr Stuart

Many people who came into contact with the Stuarts did not hide their dislike for the way in which they demanded unconditional deference from the Germans and their own side. Margaret Osborne, one of the CORB escorts wrote in a letter:

> On board we have a very dangerous couple, a man and wife who were the only first class passengers on our ship and who have made us all ashamed of them by their disgusting behaviour as prisoners both to us and to the Germans. He is a Magistrate and is being transferred from one spot to another and she writes. They are both out and out rotters and as he has a certain power, very dangerous people to give evidence too. Since the shelling they have labelled every one of us, and told other folks the most degrading things about us escorts. They are both quite certainly unbalanced, possibly the shelling had something to do with it, although they were completely unscathed, but our officers say that they were a bit batty before. He was taken to task by the officer and told that if the Germans could respect and honour British women, he certainly should, and that if his rudeness was repeated he would be locked below. In their position they could have been such a

> good example and help to us, instead of making us ashamed to be their fellow prisoners.

Personal hygiene was clearly a major problem on the raiders and the majority made some attempt at maintaining some degree of dignity. Betsy Sandbach and Geraldine Edge, both CORB escorts described how, at a Sunday morning service conducted by a still clean-shaven Father Kelly, Judge Stuart lay throughout the service under a table, unshaven and clad only in dirty pyjamas while his wife, wearing only a night-shirt which did little to protect her modesty, kicked her husband at intervals to wake him up.

Margaret Osborne continued in her letter:

> These damned Stuarts for instance have caused enough trouble to fill a book. It is a bit thick when the German officer in charge of the prisoners has to order him to get his clothes washed (he was allowed to sleep in the cabin with his wife and not be taken below with the men) and to tell him that his wife was improperly dressed. She came off our ship fully dressed and she went around in a state which I should not like to have been seen in an entirely female community, and most certainly not in front of men and children. Disgusting beast.

One might have concluded that, without the servants normally at their command, the Stuarts were unable to maintain an acceptable level of decorum. But Osborne's comment about filling a book was most prophetic. Nearly sixty years later, the Stuarts' behaviour during their time in Tonga filled up a whole chapter in a book about Queen Salote of Tonga by Elizabeth Wood-Ellem. She describes how, as Chief Justice, Chief Magistrate, Judge of Land Court, Privy Councillor and member of the Government in Parliament, Stuart not only had no regard for others but 'Failed to uphold the dignity of office, attending Supreme Court in dirty shorts and even dirtier shoes.' After two years of a three year contract, the Stuarts had caused serious divisions at the highest levels in the Tongan government, legislature, culture and society. The reason that the Stuarts were on *Rangitane* was because the Colonial Office had finally acceded to Queen Salote's continuing demands that Stuart be removed from office. Quite simply he had been sacked. Unfortunately, the Colonial Office closed ranks and cloaked his removal to such an extent that Stuart truly believed that his transfer to become Second Puisne Judge in British Guiana was a reward for his good work in Tonga.

With so much time on their hands, the prisoners entertained themselves as best they could. Some played cards - particularly cribbage, using cards and cribbage board that one popular crew member had the foresight to pack before evacuating *Rangitane*. Others recounted stories or described the first meal they would order in a restaurant on their release. Somebody had rescued his accordion which was a mixed blessing because he only knew, and repeated many times, the same few tunes. Margaret Osborne penned a poem as a tribute to those who died during the attack:

Through the grey quiet of a November dawn
The Rangitane sails upon her homeward way,
When, suddenly, a shadow deep appears
And takes its shape in the uprising day.

A foreign ship! The bridge springs to life.
The Captain wakens from his well earned sleep.
A second ship has now appeared in view
Is it an enemy upon the ocean deep?

As soon as born, our fears turn certainties,
The wireless message which we try to send
Wakens the guns upon the savage foe
And with shrill cries, the call of wild voices blend.

The cruel shells piercing the ship's stout frame

Have daunted not one man's determined mind
To send that message - though it should cost their life
To save all men and ships who sail behind.

The ship manoeuvres to protect her guns,
Relentlessly the shells still pierce her side.
Below the passengers with quiet calm
In darkness, amidst roaring tumult glide.

At last, from fire, blast of flood and smoke
Respite is gained. There falls a sudden hush
The guns are silent. Strangest sounds are heard
Men's voices calling: waters suddenly rush.

The gurgling breathing of a dying girl
The joke upon the lips of one who is
Grievously wounded, even unto death,
And yet has light and laughter in her eyes.

At last the order 'Take to the boats' rings out
Obediently with perfect calm, each one
Goes to his place: the boats swing out and down,
The ship now floats, afire, her duty done.

In her, our friends and loved ones find a grave
For England's love and England's life they died.
We left them there and prayed the mighty sea
Would welcome them - their earthly bodies hide.

We love them still - but cannot hold regret,
They would have chosen to make that sacrifice.
If they had known that their death could save
Others, freely would they have given their life.

For some it was death, others were prisoners taken,
Each, in his way, has survived his country's ends.
Again will do so as long as England needs
Ships and the sea. On these her life depends.

Margaret Osborne was quite pleased with what she had written and asked Captain Upton whether he would be proud if she managed to get it published as a tribute to those who died. Captain Upton replied 'Miss Osborne, I am very proud of it already. How much more proud I will be if you get it printed.'

In England, the New Zealand Shipping Company received a telegram on 28 November confirming *Rangitane*'s loss and asking them to inform relatives. Harold Cookson's mother was sent a letter on 3 December to say that that her son was on *Rangitane* which was presumed lost due to an enemy and that there had been no news of survivors. The letter added some crumbs of comfort by saying that crews of ships sunk by similar raiders had been set free and rescued or had been taken prisoner. This was the official line taken in the first official statement given to the international press which only referred to the loss of a British ship in New Zealand waters without publishing any names. It was not until New Year's Day that the full story was to break to the world. Frank Cookson's family were kept well informed by the shipping company and later by the Red Cross. On the 10 January 1941 they received a telegram from the company to say that he had been detained on an enemy raider and a letter in June to say that he was a POW in Stalag XB in Germany.

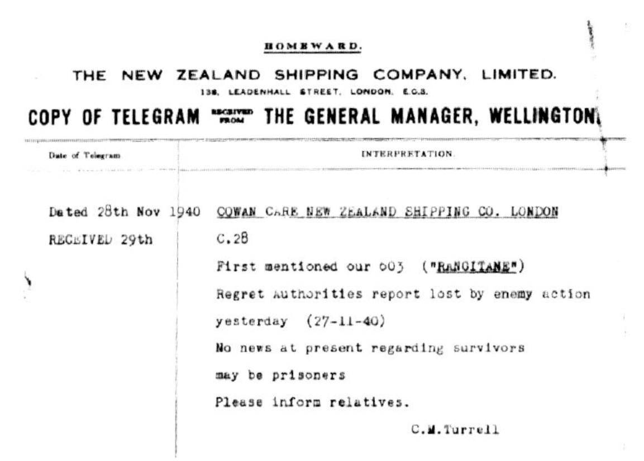

HOMEWARD.

THE NEW ZEALAND SHIPPING COMPANY, LIMITED.

138, LEADENHALL STREET, LONDON, E.C.3.

COPY OF TELEGRAM RECEIVED FROM THE GENERAL MANAGER, WELLINGTON.

Date of Telegram	INTERPRETATION.
Dated 28th Nov 1940 RECEIVED 29th	COWAN CARE NEW ZEALAND SHIPPING CO. LONDON C.28 First mentioned our 003 ("RANGITANE") Regret Authorities report lost by enemy action yesterday (27-11-40) No news at present regarding survivors may be prisoners Please inform relatives. C.M.Turrell

When Frank Ellison's mother received her first telegram she refused to accept that Frank was dead; one day she said 'We will hear from our Frank soon' - and she eventually did when a photograph of Frank in POW camp was organised and sent by the Red Cross in 1941. Johnny Thompson's grandmother remembered waking from a nightmare about Johnny in his pyjamas on a sinister black ship: this was before she had been told of the sinking and of Orion's nick-name of 'The Black Raider.' Johnny's family also received a photograph organised by the Red Cross.

Chapter 6

The journey to Nauru

It became evident to the raider commanders that the prisoners were to be a problem. Not only had they picked up over 330 survivors in the last few days, there was the question of accommodating men and women separately. In the early afternoon of 29 November, in sight of the island of Raoul in the Kermadac islands, the three ships closed up and the captains went aboard *Kulmerland* for a conference. It was decided that the prisoners had to be released as soon as possible on an island with food and water and sufficiently far away to delay their repatriation. It is evident that there was disagreement between Eyssen and Weyher about who should be released: Eyssen wanted to land everybody but Weyher only wanted to release non-Europeans and to transport the remainder back to POW camp in Germany. Weyher believed that the professional seamen knew too much about the raiders and, if released, would be able to give valuable information to the British authorities and could join the fight against Germany. It seems surprising that the famous German efficiency did not have formal policy on how to deal with such a situation. However, it was agreed that the raiders should head for the British island of Nauru which was a major supplier of phosphates, attack any ships there and release the prisoners. The plan was for *Sparrow*, *Komet's* plane, to reconnoitre Nauru to find out which ships were there and to find a safe landing place for the prisoners.

The captains' choice of Nauru is interesting: it was a major supplier of phosphates for fertiliser but there was also an old score to settle. Nauru is a tiny island of only eight square miles which was incorporated into the German Marshall Islands in

1888. It was not until 1899 that the value of the phosphate reserves was assessed by a British prospecting company. Full scale mining and export started soon after. Shortly after the outbreak of WWI, Australia sent HMAS *Melbourne* to capture Nauru on behalf of the British government. Great Britain, Australia and New Zealand were given a joint League of Nations mandate over Nauru following the Treaty of Versailles and Australia became responsible for the island's administration. Three commissioners, one from each country, were appointed to control the phosphate business on Nauru and another smaller phosphate reserve on Ocean Island, 150 miles to the east. A valuable business grew over the next twenty years. Nauru lacked a natural harbour and the commissioners invested in deep water anchorages and cantilever loading facilities. As well as chartering bulk carrier ships, the company bought four phosphate ships, the *Triona*, *Triadic*, *Triaster* and *Trienza*, the '*Tri*' prefix representing the constituent government triumvirate. By 1940 about 1.5 million tons of phosphate was shipped from Nauru and Ocean islands and Eyssen believed that it had all been stolen from Germany. While the three raiders would not be able to recapture the island for the Fatherland, at least they could leave it with a bloody nose as a token reprisal. Eyssen recorded his delight at having captured a 1932 version of the 'Pacific Islands Pilot' and a 1938 navigation chart on *Rangitane* which would help him get to Nauru. Their plan was to reach Nauru by dawn on the 8 December.

Before setting off, it was decided to redistribute some of the prisoners between the three ships. As well as making it easier to accommodate all the women on one ship, it was considered more appropriate to put the women and children on the unarmed *Kulmerland*. Captain Eyssen was clearly uneasy about having women and children on his warship. Shortly after, motor launches transferred all but one of the women and children together with husbands and fathers to *Kulmerland* and some of the *Kulmerland* men to *Komet*. The engineering officers imprisoned on *Kulmerland* were reunited with Captain Upton and his officers on *Komet.* However, one woman could not transfer to *Kulmerland*: Florence Mundie had been seriously injured in the face and needed the better medical attention available on *Komet.* Eyssen said that the women and children were unhappy at moving to another ship, but the children particularly were persuaded with the help of a bar of chocolate each. The German captains also traded equipment: *Kulmerland* received thirty-five bunks to accommodate the women and children in greater comfort, while brand new plates, mugs and cutlery were shared between the other ships. Eyssen noted in his diary that he would need to tighten security to avoid rebellion now that he had a large number of young 'fighting men' on his ship. The three raiders finally set off at 6 p.m. on Friday 29 November, steering a course of 330° for Nauru.

During the journey to Nauru, Eyssen was able to evaluate the documents seized from *Holmwood* and *Rangitane.* His diary records his delight at finding a copy of all admiralty instructions to merchant shipping between 27 August and the end of November 1939. 'SKL' (German naval command) 'will be pleased!' he recorded in his diary.

After the traumatic events of the previous few days, life became quiet and repetitive for a week. The women on *Kulmerland*, many of whom had been evacuated in their nightwear, kept themselves busy making new clothes and even formed a choir group. The crew on *Orion* were busy changing the ship's disguise again: *Orion's* success in the previous months meant that too many survivors knew what she looked like. Earlier attempts at disguise had involved removing her forward masts so these were replaced with replicas made of matchboard and canvas. When Weyher decided on the Japanese *Maebasi Maru* disguise, nobody on *Orion* knew how to paint the name in Japanese characters. In desperation they even considered copying some script from a Kodak advert in a Japanese magazine, but wondered whether their ship would then be called 'super-sensitive' or 'exposure'. On *Komet*, Eyssen carried out a detailed analysis of the benefit of disrupting the Nauru phosphate trade, arguing that it would seriously affect agricultural production for the allies. He did not appear too worried when his Arado plane, *Sparrow* sank, because it was unreliable and only capable of being used for four days during the previous eight weeks.

Roy Poole, *Rangitane's* third officer, recalled in 1980 that the prisoners on *Komet* were woken daily at about 6 a.m. to martial music, and entertained most evenings by records and German radio programmes broadcast over the ship's tannoy. While Lord Haw Haw's propaganda programmes were a source of wry amusement, the prisoners collapsed in hilarity when the *Komet* crew played records captured from *Rangitane*, particularly when recordings of 'Adolf - you have bitten off more than you can chew' and 'Run rabbit' were played inadvertently. The *Komet* crew also published a typewritten news sheet called 'Wireless news for passengers' which gave the latest German version of the progress of the war.

On Thursday 5 December the three ships again stopped in the twilight and the captains met to review their strategy and arrangements for attacking Nauru and landing the prisoners. They had received intelligence reports that a British cruiser had left the Japan area on 28 November and was heading for Australia, probably in response to the loss of *Rangitane*. Eyssen said that there was a small chance that it may travel via Nauru and cause them a problem, but it was not sufficiently dangerous to abandon their plans. The captains made a social occasion of their meeting, particularly exchanging mementos of their adventures. Eyssen gave Weyher a framed picture found on *Rangitane* of the *SS Turakina* which had been sunk by *Orion* earlier in the year. Pschunder gave Eyssen an oil painting of *Rangitane*. It is known that Eyssen sent a picture of *Rangitane* to Captain Upton after the war and it would be interesting to speculate whether this was the same picture. Unfortunately its whereabouts is not known. Just before midnight the three ships set off on the final leg of their journey to Nauru.

It is clear that Captain Upton had gained the confidence of *Komet's* Captain Eyssen. Within a few days of being captured, Upton was invited to Eyssen's cabin to share a few glasses of whiskey and cigarettes. Upton said in the 1941 inquiry that he was well aware that he was befriended so that his captors could gain advantage, but felt that he had not disclosed any sensitive information. However, it became evident over subsequent days that there were common interests and experiences. Both captains had witnessed a similar type naval warfare, but from opposite sides. Eyssen joined the Imperial Navy in 1911 and had early experience in 1914 of stalking and sinking merchant shipping off the South American coast. Although Upton did his training in the merchant navy, he was a Royal Naval Reservist in WWI. As a young Lieutenant he commanded a small flotilla of Q-ships based with the British Home Fleet at Longhope on Scapa Flow. These were mainly secretly armed fishing trawlers whose purpose was to act as decoys to locate and destroy German U-boats. While Q-ships had limited success during WWI, Upton had attracted the attention of Admiral Sir Stanley Colville, then in command of Northern Trawlers at Scapa. He was a keen supporter of decoy tactics and was clearly impressed by the way Upton had given chase to a U-boat in April 1915. In a letter to Upton's commanding officer, Colville commended Upton on the way that he had used the three boats under his command to intercept the submarine. It is somewhat ironic that twenty-five years later, Upton would himself become a victim of disguised warships. There was obviously an affinity between Eyssen and Upton which developed from professional respect to friendship that was to become a valuable asset in the following weeks. Captain Eyssen explained to Upton the difficulty of having so many prisoners to feed and stated his intention of releasing everybody on a suitable island as soon as possible. This information was disseminated to all prisoners and morale was raised significantly. Unfortunately, every sight of land was greeted with excitement that release was imminent, followed by disappointment when the land disappeared over the horizon.

Just after 9 a.m. on the Friday 6th December, a loud radio message was intercepted. *Komet* and *Kulmerland* were despatched to investigate the identity of the ship which turned out to be the American freighter *Clevedon.* Being a neutral ship, *Kulmerland* and *Komet* returned to their original course for Nauru. At about the same time *Orion* saw heavy smoke about 20 miles away on the port quarter. Sometime later, Weyher became concerned that the ship may also be travelling to Nauru, would see the three raiders and might warn the authorities. He turned *Orion* hard to port towards the unknown ship and gradually built up to full-speed. He informed *Komet* and *Kulmerland* of the quarry's speed and direction and arranged for them to move to an attacking position.

Little did Weyher know that he was to meet again with an old foe. Back in August *Orion* had been hunting the Pacific trade routes with little success. On 10 August Weyher saw the MV *Triona*, a phosphate ship, off Brisbane. When *Triona*'s captain realised that he was in danger he reversed course at full speed. *Orion* could have given chase but it was late afternoon and the chances of catching up within attacking distance before dark were slim. It was amazing that *Triona* had not broadcast a raider warning message. Weyher decided not to push his luck but he was irritated that *Triona* had slipped through his fingers. Now, in December, Lieutenant Bürbheim on *Orion* told his captain that the unknown ship was the *Triona* again. Weyher was delighted but knew that he would have to exercise caution, knowing that *Triona*'s captain was not stupid. *Triona* was clearly on its way to Nauru and had to be stopped before she raised the alarm.

At ten miles distance and heading straight for *Triona*, *Orion* presented only her bow view and could not readily be identified. There was intermittent low cloud and rain around and *Komet* and *Kulmerland* had disappeared from view. *Orion*, mainly hidden in rain, was now astern of *Triona* which was travelling north. *Komet* and *Kulmerland* were still hidden in the low cloud north of *Triona*. But Weyher couldn't take action until he knew exactly where *Komet* was. Finally, the cloud lifted for a short time and *Komet* was directly in front of *Triona* and *Orion* was behind. Weyher's old foe was trapped. At 5.20 p.m. *Komet* fired a warning shot and signalled *Triona* to stop and not to use her radio. *Triona* immediately tried to transmit a QQQQ raider warning and her position. The signal was immediately drowned by *Orion's* radio operator who transmitted a strong false Japanese signal on the same frequency. The attack then started in earnest: *Triona*, which by this time had started zigzagging in and out of low cloud, had to be stopped at all costs. Both *Komet* and *Orion* opened fire with their six-inch guns and soon found their range. After over nine hours, *Triona* finally surrendered and lowered her boats. Three Filipino and Chinese had been killed, many more injured. The survivors of the sixty-four crew and seven passengers made their way to the raiders. By nightfall the prize crews had completed their search and had restocked the raiders' depleted larders with fruit, vegetables, drink and tobacco. Pineapples, oranges, tomatoes and salad were obviously a special treat to the *Komet* crew, but particular delight was expressed at having obtained cucumbers. Eyssen also recorded that they had found women's clothes in Christmas presents being sent to Nauru. These, he thought, would be useful if they came across another passenger ship which needed to be evacuated quickly with women still in their nightclothes. He dryly commented that, for the time being, the women of Nauru would have to dress modestly without their new clothes. Eyssen also regretted that he did not have more time to explore the *Triona* which he described as being a clean and tidy vessel.

Triona was a nine year old, 4,413 ton freighter belonging to the British Phosphate Commissioners and was transporting 1,112 tons of food and materials from Newcastle in New South Wales to Nauru. She was sunk by a single torpedo at 10.54 p.m. at 5° 12' S, 165° 39' E.

The raiders headed north at top speed. They were now close to Nauru and tension had been heightened by their encounter with *Triona*. It took some time to analyse various papers found on board, including 'the whole post office' being delivered to Nauru. This included many personal letters which Eyssen said would still be delivered to their recipients: 'It's the least I can do' he wrote in his diary. Little new intelligence was gained from the *Triona* crew; the only item recorded in Weyher's diary was that new Admiralty orders required all ships to maintain lookouts in the crow's nest. The crew said that they thought *Orion* was a ship they had expected to see from Nauru and couldn't understand why she was on a strange course. Among the survivors were five women, one being a mother from Nauru with her eighteen year old daughter. They were returning from a Christmas shopping trip in Melbourne: they had lost all of their festive provisions and presents. Weyher recorded that the women were initially fearsome of the reputation of the German raiders but that they soon found that they were treated with real consideration. He said that they were particularly interested in the German women's fashion magazines which just happened to be lying around on *Orion*. Evidence presented to the 1941 official inquiry said that the December shipping schedule was in the post captured on *Triona*. Eyssen would have known about the number and type of ships to be expected at Nauru.

The logistics of off-loading so many captives onto a small Pacific island were daunting. It was known that Nauru had no natural harbour or jetty suitable for mooring and it was clear that every prisoner would have to be taken by motor launch to the shore, together with sufficient provisions to last several days before help could arrive. But there had also been a major disagreement between Captains Eyssen and Weyher over who should be released and who should be retained in captivity. Eyssen wanted to release everybody; he argued that the drain on the raiders' limited resources would be unacceptable and would hamper their mission. Weyher was adamant that only women, children and non-Europeans should be released. He could not accept that anybody in the armed forces should be released to fight another day or that merchant seamen would be released to help re-supply a beleaguered Britain. How exactly the two captains finally settled on the solution is not clear and neither captain makes any more than a passing comment on the issue in their war diaries. It is evident however that Captain Upton's tact and diplomacy was used in horse-trading to try to get as many prisoners released as possible. Whose idea it was, is not known, but it was agreed that, apart from the RNZAF men on *Komet* who were to be transferred to *Orion*, and three injured prisoners who would be transferred from *Orion*, everybody from *Komet* and *Kulmerland* and all non-Europeans on *Orion* were to be released. This would leave eighty-four prisoners from *Rangitane* on *Orion* together with nearly seventy from other ships. But there was a condition: all male Europeans to be released were required to sign a parole declaration.

There was much debate among the prisoners about the wisdom of agreeing to these terms. Tom Newland, one of the New Zealand Fleet Air Arm recruits, initially wanted nothing to do with such an unpatriotic promise but Upton said that he would be mad to refuse. He signed up, the general consensus being that if Captain Upton, as a decorated officer and ADC, was going to sign it, then everybody should. With typical German efficiency, prisoners had to sign five copies of their parole agreement. One signed copy is still in the possession of descendants of Lionel Upton. There was to be considerable debate many months later about the legal legitimacy of the parole and whether they should be allowed to re-engage in the war effort without reprisal.

WE THE UNDERSIGNED DO HEREBY GIVE OUR WORD OF HONOUR AND DECLARE SOLEMNLY THAT ON OUR RELEASE WE WILL BEAR NEITHER ARMS NOR UNDER= TAKE MILITARY ACTIONS AGAINST GERMANY AND HER ALLIES DURING THE PRESENT HOSTILITIES! BY BREACH OF THIS PROMISE WE REALISE WE ARE LIABLE TO CAPITAL PUNISHMENT!

Ex " M.V. "Rangitane"

1. Capt. H.L.Upton ....
2. Ch.Offic.E.Hopkins ....
3. 2nd. " H.St.Williams ....
4. 3rd. " R.Poole ....
5. 4th. " R.G.Taylor ....

What is amazing is that only two of the Fleet Air Arm recruits were interned. They were Jack Dark and Mac Dowding who were on *Orion* under Weyher's stricter regime. All the others were to be released by Eyssen from *Komet*. Eyssen got his way in disposing of all of his prisoners while Captain Weyher partly got his way by retaining 150 potential combatants for forward transit to POW camp in Germany. It is probable that this disagreement over the release of prisoners was a final straw for Eyssen: he records being tired of his squadron, particularly *Orion's* continuing mechanical problems hindering progress. He decided that, after discharging all of his prisoners, he would operate independently, leaving Weyher to live with the problem of his unreliable vessel and how to deal with *Orion's* prisoners. There is also evidence that SKL, the German naval command, became involved with the dispute, apparently agreeing with Weyher that potential combatants should be interned. SKL followed this up by issuing an instruction to all raiders, clearly aimed at Eyssen, about the future handling of prisoners. Eyssen was displeased and it did not help relations with Weyher.

All of *Orion*'s prisoners were understandably unhappy that they were not to be released. For many it had been their misfortune to be captive on *Orion* and subject to the harsher Weyher regime; had they been imprisoned on *Komet* or *Kulmerland*, they may have been preparing for their release. In particular, the RNZAF men were unhappy at being detained and implored Captains Upton and Miller to lobby the Germans on their behalf:

> 6/12/40
> To Captain Eyssen
> Sir,
> On behalf of the fifteen members of the Royal New Zealand RAF (Wireless Section) we beg to request that you might see your way to reconsider your decision to intern them. They all give their Word of Honour that they will leave the Service, and we feel positive that the Government of New Zealand would release them. Captain Miller and my General Manager in New Zealand would see the Minister concerned regarding their release from military service. You will possibly have other members of the New Zealand RAF as hostages in the future. In the event of this request meeting with your approval may we specially stress the cases of Harden, Shaw, Kimberley and Allan who are listed with the Air Force but have had no training of any description and have not been attested or taken the Oath of Allegiance.
> Signed by Captains Upton and Miller

The request was refused and the RNZAF men sat out the war in a number of POW camps in Germany. Jack Almond, Third Electrical Officer told the story that one unnamed *Komet* prisoner was selected for detention. He was actually a *Rangitane* passenger but was suspected by the Germans to be a soldier. In desperation he pointed to his obvious glass eye and said that it proved his civilian status. The gravity of the situation was lightened when a German jokingly asked if anybody had ever heard of Nelson. It worked: the person involved was to be released. Almond also reported that one key person was in danger of not being released - Captain Upton. As well as being in the Royal Naval Reserve, he was also an ADC to King George VI. Upton later reported that, although Eyssen discovered these facts, he agreed to release him saying '... I will get into much trouble with Goering or the Reich when I get back.'

Other preparations were made for the landing. Eyssen had promised a boat, kerosene and food. Dr. Crawford, *Rangitane's* surgeon, was given the medical histories of all those who had received treatment on the raiders so that they could be passed on. Sculleryman Richard Thorpe had to make 300 wooden spoons for use ashore: the raiders wanted to keep as much hardware as possible for future prisoners. In his efficient way, Captain Upton made all the preparations for landing at Nauru. But he also displayed his gentlemanly nature: he and Captain Miller wrote a letter:

> 6/12/40
> To Captain Eyssen
> Sir,
> On behalf of our ships' companies, we wish to thank you and your Officers and crew for the way we have been treated on board your ship as prisoners. Everything possible has been done for us in the circumstances and we have received all considerations. The issue of cool clothing and tobacco was most considerate and everything was done for the sick and wounded.
> Signed by Captain Upton and Captain Miller

All of these preparations were to be in vain. With Nauru less than a day away and with everybody's spirits lifting, the weather started to deteriorate and the raiders' plans were to be temporarily suspended.

Chapter 7

Nauru Island

On the afternoon of Saturday 7 December, *Komet* was within sight of Nauru and the prisoners again became excited at the thought of imminent release. There was a fresh wind of five knots, a deep swell, heavy cloud and gusts of rain. *Komet* approached from the south and saw a ship to the southeast and another to the northwest of the island, obviously drifting and waiting to load phosphates. On approaching the island, Eyssen was surprised to see how modern and large the phosphate handling facilities were. It was clear that Nauru had a much larger operation than previously believed, with modern administration buildings and neat houses. Moving *Komet* closer, Eyssen then saw another ship about five miles away to the northeast, and decided to investigate. He knew that he could return for the other two ships but thought that this third ship was under way and needed to be challenged immediately.

That ship was the Norwegian motor vessel *Vinni*, on charter to the British Phosphate Commissioners, and had left Dunedin on 21 November bound for Nauru. She had arrived on 30 November and for a week had been drifting 20 miles off Nauru waiting for an opportunity to load. She had sailed back to within five miles of the shore and had stopped engines for the night, intending to start loading the following morning. *Vinni's* Captain Helmer Henriksen reported seeing an unknown ship travelling towards his position but, being bow-on, he couldn't see its markings or flag. He was somewhat surprised when eventually he saw *Komet's* Japanese markings. He expressed his concerns to his first officer, Aslak Jensen, but was not particularly worried because he had not received any warning signal either from the strange ship or from the Nauru wireless office. His complacency was soon shattered when, less than two miles away, the ship signalled by Aldis lamp for *Vinni* to stop and not to use the radio. Henriksen immediately ordered the engines to be re-started and *Vinni* moved painfully slowly westwards around the north side of the island. It was clear that *Vinni* could not escape and Henriksen ordered his vessel to be stopped and to allow *Komet's* prize crew to come aboard.

As with the *Holmwood*, *Vinni* was taken without any QQQQ warning being broadcast. The three other ships known to be off Nauru had no idea that there were surface raiders only a few miles away. Eyssen's prize crew quickly searched *Vinni*, transferred thirty-two new prisoners to *Komet*, set explosive charges and abandoned the ship to her fate. Eyssen recorded that *Vinni* exploded in the late evening with a brilliant flash and sank only about five miles off Nauru, yet the explosion was not seen ashore. *Vinni*'s Captain Henriksen and his crew could not believe their luck when they learnt that they were all to be released the following day on Nauru. There was evidently a degree of humour between victor and vanquished: Henriksen asked Eyssen for a signed receipt to prove to his employers that Vinni was captured and sunk. Eyssen obliged and the receipt is preserved for posterity at the Norwegian Maritime Museum in Oslo.

That night all three German ships sailed twenty miles west of Nauru and the captains met just after midnight for another conference and to give the landing parties their instructions on releasing the prisoners. But *Vinni*'s captain told Eyssen that landing at Nauru was impossible with the prevailing wind causing a deep swell and breaking waves. Eyssen and Weyher decided to delay a decision until they could assess the weather condition the following day. They then agreed a plan to attack the other phosphate ships in the morning half-light: *Komet* was to round Nauru to the north and *Orion* and *Kulmerland* to the south. The attack was to start at 6.30 a.m. Weyher's diary records that he had to insist that only one raider's boarding party was to go on each captured ship. He said that after *Orion* had taken *Triona* on the previous day, *Komet* had also wanted to put a prize crew on board which he said was unacceptable. The relationship between Eyssen and Weyher was clearly deteriorating. It was becoming progressively more difficult for the two commanders to work together and to share their 'kills' in the success statistics.

At 2.00 a.m. on Sunday 8 December, the raiders parted and steamed eastwards to their rendezvous at first light. At 3.30 a.m. *Orion*'s Captain Weyher first saw a brightly lit vessel to the east of Nauru and then another to the north-east. He started closing on the first ship and, when just over a mile away, signalled asking for her identity. There was no reply; the watch was oblivious of the presence of the raider, so a warning shot was fired across the bows. This had an immediate effect - the lights were extinguished and the ship started to move away from *Orion*. The other vessel to the north-east also turned off its lights. *Orion*'s searchlights illuminated the first ship and Weyher could clearly see a stern gun, proving that it was not an independent country's trader. It took just four shells from *Orion* to stop the ship which turned out to be the 6,378 ton *SS Triadic* owned by the British Phosphate Commissioners. Captain Callender of the *Triadic* told the official inquiry that the second and third shots destroyed the wireless cabin and that luckily the wireless officer was off duty at the time. Again, no raider warning was transmitted. By the time the lifeboats were lowered, *Triadic* was ablaze and it was obviously only a matter of time before she would sink. Weyher signalled to *Kulmerland* to stop and pick up survivors while *Orion* set off to chase the other ship she had seen.

Meanwhile, Captain Eyssen on *Komet* had already seen the second ship's running lights but decided not start an attack before the pre-arranged time. He stopped his engines intending to wait until dawn, but the vessel suddenly switched its lights off and started steaming eastwards. Eyssen was in a dilemma: if he gave chase he would be travelling straight into *Orion* who was circumnavigating the island in the opposite direction and it did not need the two of them to capture the fleeing vessel. Eyssen decided to turn around and sail westwards again to take a closer look at the landing facilities on the west side of Nauru. This was a strange decision: Eyssen knew that there were three ships waiting off the eastern side of Nauru, yet he preferred to go and survey landing places. Whatever the reason, he concluded that a landing was still not possible and continued around the south of the island to survey the south and east coasts more carefully. When he arrived on the east side, *Komet* stopped and picked up a lifeboat from *Triadic*. Its occupants were furious, wanting to know why they had been attacked without warning, especially with ordinary passengers on board. Since Eyssen had not been involved in the attack and did not know what warning, if any, Weyher had given, he asked why *Triadic* was carrying passengers if it was armed with a stern gun.

At 9.45 a.m., just as everybody was back on board *Komet*, another ship was spotted to the south-east. It was the 4,165 ton *SS Komata* owned by the Union Steam Ship Company of New Zealand. She had sailed from Auckland to Suva and then on to Nauru. She had been lying overnight twenty-five miles off Nauru and was on her approach in extremely limited visibility. *Komata*'s Captain Fish saw two ships on his starboard bow and told the 1941 inquiry that he had reason to be suspicious following a report from the Nauru radio operator that there might have been a distress call earlier that morning. The operator had also transmitted a request for some ships with Japanese markings sailing off Nauru to identify themselves. When Fish saw that one of the ships in front of him was carrying Japanese flags he immediately ordered *Komata* to port and rang for full speed. *Komet,* the closer of the two suspicious ships, immediately started to close in and gave the signal by flag to stop and not to use the radio. Fish did not bother trying to decode the flag signal but ordered his radio officer to send the standard raider warning message. The signal was immediately jammed by *Komet*'s powerful radio, so Fish ordered a distress message to be sent. This was met with a barrage of shellfire: at three-quarters of a mile range, *Komata* was immediately hit on the port wing of the bridge, destroying her radio and antennae, killing the chief officer and seriously injuring the second officer, who later died. Captain Fish stopped his ship and ordered his crew to abandon as quickly as possible. He said that he packed all confidential material on the bridge into a weighted bag and threw it overboard. It is unfortunate that, immediately before being killed, the chief officer had been given the keys and instructed to dispose of all the papers in the safe in the captain's quarters. The keys, the only set available, were lost and the safe was found intact by *Komet*'s prize crew, yielding its secrets later that day. The *Komata* crew were given plenty of time to collect their personal possessions and by 2 p.m. were meeting their fellow prisoners in *Komet*'s holds.

Orion meanwhile had been in pursuit of her other quarry. Despite her troublesome engines, *Orion* made twelve knots and gradually reduced the distance, making excessive smoke to shroud her progress, much to the discomfort of her deck crew and gunners. *Orion* opened fire at a range of four miles with four shells which straddled the evading ship. This was obviously enough: the ship stopped and her lifeboats were lowered. She was *SS Triaster*, another British Phosphate Commissioners ship, whose sixty-four crew including Captain A. Rhoades were quickly imprisoned on *Orion*. There is no record of a raider warning having been transmitted. *Triaster* was scuttled by explosives placed in her holds. Weyher records with wry amusement that some of his prize crew were still on *Triaster* when the first detonation in the forward hold occurred. The ship rocked and tilted to starboard, unfooting the crew who all rushed to the stern where their motorboat was tethered. One of the crew misjudged the gap between *Triaster* and the motorboat and fell in the water. Another huge explosion shook the atmosphere and *Triaster* sank gracefully, bows first. Weyher recorded that just as the bridge reached the water, the compressed air siren let out a final grim lament.

Orion returned to the blazing *Triadic* which resolutely refused to sink. Despite the poor visibility, Weyher was worried that the smoke would be seen from Nauru. He was also aware that the Nauru radio operator was getting suspicious about lack of contact with the various ships waiting to load. He decided not to waste time and used one of *Orion*'s precious torpedoes to sink *Triadic*. Even a gaping hole did not sink the ship and Weyher had to send a demolition party to attach an explosive charge to the outside of the hull. Finally, *Triadic* gave up and sank.

In less than twenty-four hours, four phosphate ships had been sunk and hundreds more prisoners had been stowed on the raiders. It was a very depressing day for the existing prisoners: they had been expecting their imminent release on Nauru, their spirits had been high and there had been excitement in the air. In reality they had to listen to the straining engines, the deafening roar of the guns and the footsteps of yet more prisoners. Everybody knew from their own recent experience what the crew and passengers on the attacked ships were going through. The final straw was when everybody was told that the weather conditions were too bad to allow them to land at Nauru for several days.

On *Orion* there was a sad act for the *Rangitane* survivors: James McNulty, a thirty-year old merchant seaman from Bristol, died from injuries sustained during the shelling of *Rangitane*. Captain Weyher recorded how his medical team had fought to save him but his heart had finally failed. His body was draped with the Union flag and he was committed to the sea.

The 1941 official inquiry was amazed that the authorities on Nauru were completely oblivious to the presence of the raiders. They had been within only a few miles of the shore for most of the previous afternoon and evening and had attacked and sunk three ships the following day. The Nauru radio operator had been heard by the raiders asking its neighbour, Ocean Island, whether they had heard a distress signal and later, asking the Japanese ships to identify themselves. This implies that they had actually seen the raiders with the Japanese insignia. Eyssen noted that Nauru was illuminated as if electricity was free and *Triadic* and *Triaster* had been observed with full running lights. It is known that *Komata* made a distress signal which had first been jammed by *Komet* and later had been overlaid by contrived responses from *Komet*. The Ocean Island radio operator had clearly been uneasy at the confused jammed message yet the Nauru operator appears to have been appeased by the false *Komet* messages. Nauru tried several times to raise *Triona*, *Triadic* and *Triaster* but, according to Weyher, *Komet*'s operators managed to maintain a credible charade.

Over the next few weeks there were many allegations of enemy spies operating on and signalling the Germans about the ships currently waiting off Nauru. The intelligence services carried out at least three separate investigations arising from tip-offs. The most credible story was told by Mrs. Lorna Adams, a survivor of *Triona*, to Captain Upton and later to investigators. She said that Thomas Hudson, a mechanic on Ocean Island, had confessed while drunk that he was on secret service for a middle-European country. Hudson was very friendly with Eric Paul on Nauru. He was under separate investigation because of alleged misuse of confidential shipping movement records as revealed in inter-island correspondence intercepted by the censor. Paul had been appointed from outside the community as a confidential clerk to the local phosphate company manager and was responsible for transmitting ship movement information to other company offices. He was also the local representative of the Navy Office who had sole control over the wireless installation as part of the wartime control orders. Unfortunately, he was universally disliked for being too authoritarian and having been appointed over the heads of local candidates who considered themselves more qualified for his job. Being in total control of ship movement information, Paul became the butt of gossip and rumour when he allegedly refused to warn local shipping about suspicious events off Nauru.

These investigations merged into one. It transpired that Mrs. Adams had had an affair with Hudson which turned sour. Mr. Adams had agreed to a divorce so Mrs. Adams could marry Hudson; unfortunately for Mrs. Adams, Hudson didn't want to leave his wife and he ended the affair. Then the recriminations started, culminating in Mrs. Adams making fanciful allegations about Hudson being a foreign agent working with Eric Paul. The investigators understandably concluded that there was no basis to the allegations other than a local love-tryst getting out of hand. Eric Paul had been dragged in simply because nobody liked him and he was too friendly with Hudson.

A third investigation was relatively short-lived. A Mr. Kidd, in a moment of drunken madness, bragged to his drinking partners that he knew who was responsible for the shipping losses off Nauru. When challenged, he theatrically dictated an urgent telegram to the defence department in Melbourne advising them to keep a close watch on a person named Jolly. He had been in government administration before managing a plantation in New Guinea. Kidd signed the message 'Bill' – not his own name but probably a play on the cowboy Billy the Kid. Unfortunately, the junior assistant taking the dictation thought it was a genuine message and it ended up on a security official's desk in Melbourne. The Criminal Investigation Branch took over but Kidd quickly confessed to his stupidity, admitting that Jolly, whom he had met only a couple of times many years previously, was the first name he plucked out of the air for a joke. Both Kidd and the misguided Lorna Adams had a very serious dressing down but no charges were made against them.

The weather conditions at Nauru did not improve and it was clear to Eyssen that he would have to abandon temporarily his plans to land the prisoners. Another problem had been preying on his mind for some time: *Komet* was running low on supplies, particularly fuel and food and it was now an opportune time to replenish from *Kulmerland.* But the weather conditions would not allow *Komet* and *Kulmerland* to raft together to transfer the supplies safely. It was agreed that *Komet* and *Kulmerland* would sail 510 miles to Ailinglaplap atoll in the Marshall Islands while *Orion* was to patrol Ponape. The German captains planned to meet up again on Friday 13 November just north of Nauru to attempt another landing to release the prisoners.

Ailinglaplap is a group of fifty-six islets surrounding a lagoon of about 300 square miles. As part of the Marshall Islands, it was annexed by Germany in 1885 but ceded to Japan in 1914 becoming a Japanese mandated territory in 1920. Ailinglaplap had previously been used by *Orion* to refuel from the supply ship *Regensburg.* The prisoners on *Komet* and *Kulmerland* were not very happy with their change of circumstances. Having been told of their imminent release, they now knew that they were steaming north towards less friendly territories. On Wednesday, 11 December the routine on *Komet* was broken by a loud crash: while coming alongside *Kulmerland*, the deep swell had caused the gunwales and guard rails to clash, causing some damage. When the prisoners were eventually allowed on deck they found that they were in an atoll which, had it not been for their circumstances, would have been idyllic.

Re-provisioning took longer than expected. *Komet* and *Kulmerland* were to have met up with *Orion* on the thirteenth, but on that day they were still at Ailinglaplap. During this time *Orion* had been bobbing around in the continuing atrocious weather around Nauru. Force eleven gales were still blowing. Captain Weyher had learnt from some of the Nauru prisoners that there was a sheltered bay on the north of Nauru which was usually approachable, even in bad weather. The bay was the location of a leper colony and, a few hundred yards away, there was a settlement of native fishermen who would usually transfer passengers from ship to shore. The bay was located on the charts but no action could be taken until *Orion* met up again with the other ships from Ailinglaplap. The three ships eventually came together on Monday 16 December just north of Nauru, to review the situation. The weather was still bad and the outlook no better. *Orion* was still plagued by engine problems and it was finally decided to abandon the Nauru landing.

It is not clear from either Eyssen's or Weyher's diaries why they chose to head for the tiny island of Emirau in the Bismarck Archipelago, over 1000 miles away. It is obvious that their choice was not random because their course from Nauru was precise and unwavering. Geoffrey Barley, one of the *Rangitane* prisoners, claimed that Captain Eyssen had told him that he had been to Emirau (or Storm Island as it had previously been known) when it was under German control before the First World War. Eyssen recorded how magnanimous he had felt in planning to release the prisoners on an island under British control with sufficient supplies to ensure no deprivation until they could be rescued. Captain Upton had frequent conferences with Eyssen to discuss the logistics of the release and it seems inevitable that he was instrumental in negotiating supplies of food and fuel.

The raiders anchored off Emirau Island

Morale amongst the prisoners improved once again but there was much cynicism: previous plans for release had been thwarted too many times. By Sunday 20 December, hope was high; they had been sailing west for two days and in the early evening Emirau was at last within sight. But most important of all, the weather was perfect for landing and detailed arrangements were being made for disembarkation. Geoffrey Barley could not believe it when he finally saw Emirau. 'There it was - leaning palm trees with a base of thick vivid tropical greenery, and in the foreground a deep blue calm lagoon.'

Supplies of food, water and kerosene, sufficient for three days were assembled. Working parties were formed and Captain Eyssen enjoyed his moment of magnanimity, walking among his captives and declaring his delight at their imminent release. 'Tomorrow you will be drinking whisky and soda there' he would say jovially, pointing towards a small white bungalow partly hidden in Emirau's vegetation. *Rangitane*'s Dr. Crawford was given medical supplies by the German doctor, together with the medical histories of everybody who had been treated on the raiders. Barley also recorded that Eyssen said in a serious tone that he wished that he was also going with them. It is evident that there must have been a genuine respect, if not friendship, between the German and British senior officers. In 1948, one of the German Officers sent Upton a picture of the Virgin Mary, on the back of which was written:

Dear Sir!

When we saidGood Bye!" at Emirau Island Christmas 1941 we promised each other to send a little message after the war.

My Name is Werner Schulz-Heik and I was one of the young Naval Officers on board the small German Auxiliar Cruiser "Komet". I should think, You will remenber me at best if I tell You that I was the officer, who lended a small Ford lorry from Mr. Miller and brought the sick people of your RANGITANE-crew to the native village. Do you remenber, that I filmed this scene? Youself are visible on this little moving picture and I have some other snapshots which I am sure will find your interest.

Please let me know Your address so that I can send you some little souvenirs from that time, which has seen us in such a heavy fighting for our countries.

We surviving and beaten Germans try to continue our private and business existennce by heavy work - the daily conditions and circumstances are very hard, but it is our duty to stay and to hope for a better patriotic ideal, than that one, which was given us by the unqualifyable nasi-government.

I hope for a good news of you Mr. Upton
sencerely Yours

Not everybody was pleased: it was again confirmed that the prisoners on *Orion* and some New Zealand airmen on *Komet* were not to be released. Their future was very uncertain.

Chapter 8

Emirau Island

Emirau (variously known as Emir, E-Mira, Emira, Squally, Storm, Sturm, Hunter, Kerue and Beefsteak) is a tiny island of thirteen square miles in the Bismarck Archipelago, now part of New Ireland province of Papua New Guinea. Whatever its name, this small island has some history worth telling.

Its first recorded discovery was on 26 February, 1700 by Captain William Dampier who headed an expedition of discovery to New Holland and New Guinea ordered by King William III. Dampier couldn't land because of bad weather and he named it Squally Island. There were no recorded visits to the island until 1864 when labour recruiters landed to establish trading relations and were attacked, losing at least two crew members. Ships kept away until 1896 when a schooner from the New Guinea Company landed, but was repulsed by natives. A further attempt in 1898 had the same result. After the Imperial German Government took control of the area, they sent the warship *Seeadler* to the area which established cautious trading relations with the islanders. In April 1901 Bruno Mencke and his privately funded expedition arrived but after initial good relations, his large party including armed militia was attacked and he was killed on neighbouring St Matthias Island.

In 1909, a larger than life German character called Carl Leopold Bruno Wilde arrived in Rabaul as a trainee plantation manager. He was a graduate of the Hamburg School of Tropical Agriculture and had already had two failed businesses, one in Berlin and another in Czechoslovakia. He also had a failed marriage, leaving his wife and young daughter Helga in Germany. He moved to Argentina and then Sydney where he set up a motor repair business. At thirty-three years old, he started his two year contract in New Guinea to manage a plantation on Makada Island. He met and married Juanita Stehr, the daughter of the manager or owner of Manuan plantation on the Duke of York islands. Juanita was from a colourful family – she was the granddaughter of 'Queen' Emma, the powerful and beautiful woman from Samoan royalty who beguiled her way to being the populist head of the European Pacific community. Juanita was born in Australia and educated in New Zealand and therefore was a British citizen. While Wilde was working under contract at Makada, he was barred from setting up in competition with his employers so, when he and his wife discovered Emira (as Emirau was then named) plantation was for sale, they bought it in Juanita's name. In late-1912, Wilde and Juanita started establishing a large coca plantation on the island and bought a large schooner which he re-named *Emira.*

On the outbreak of the First World War Australia, New Zealand and Japan seized the German colonies and possessions in the South Pacific. The authorities tried to confiscate Emirau from Wilde and to expel him because of his German nationality. But luck was on their side: they successfully argued that Emirau was bought years earlier in Juanita's name as a British citizen and that their marriage gave Wilde the right of residency. The Wildes were left alone to build up a plantation which would employ nearly 1000 local people.

The Homestead

By the mid-1920s Wilde had created a large plantation on Emirau and had built accommodation and welfare facilities for his workers in the south-west corner of Emirau just opposite the tiny Ianusau Island. Wilde called this his Homestead. As well as large dining halls and kitchens, there were married and single men's dormitories, a large building with billiard table, tennis table, library and gym, a guesthouse with three bedrooms, bathrooms and second cookhouse. There was even a fridge capable of storing one ton of goods, and a hospital and surgery with a ward with six beds. Everything was powered by a generator providing electrically pumped running water to all buildings.

Wilde was described as 'a true Prussian, arrogant and overbearing' but he clearly made a huge success of his business. Juanita bore four children and Wilde was known to have been extremely happy with his life, describing it as idyllic. But tragedy was to strike when Juanita fell pregnant again. The pregnancy did not go well and towards the end of her term Wilde decided to take her to the hospital in Kavieng. After setting out on his schooner *Emira,* Juanita went into labour and Wilde turned back to Emirau. He helped to deliver two baby girls, Faith and Hope, but Juanita died. There is conflicting evidence about the fate of the babies: Les Bell in his marvellous account 'New Guinea Engineer' and John Meehan in a short biography of Wilde, said that one girl was stillborn and the other died shortly after. Wilde family recollections say that one baby died but the other survived, being rejected by Wilde and taken into care by German missionaries.

Wilde's schooner Emira

Juanita and one or maybe two babies were buried on Emirau close to the Homestead. With Bell's help, Wilde erected a black marble cross weighing over one ton to her memory, which still stands today. Visitors to Emirau in recent years have noted that the memorial is clearly still looked after by local people. It is known that a young native girl called Lau who nursed Wilde's other four young children continued to tend the graves until she was into old age. Peter Shanagan, one of Wilde's grandsons, recalls a story that when Lau died, she wanted to be buried next to her beloved Juanita. Wilde died in Sydney in 1950 and his ashes were taken to Emirau and scattered next to her memorial.

Wilde was devoted to Juanita and after her death he returned to Germany, clearly suffering from his grief. At some point he returned to Emirau with Helga, the daughter from his first marriage and continued with his plantation business. Wilde later sold Emirau and the plantation was eventually acquired by W R Carpenter & Co. Wilde's commercial exploits on Emirau would have been enough for any enterprising man but they pale into insignificance compared with what followed. He built up a successful coffee and gold mining business in the Wau area of what is today's Morobe province of Papua New Guinea. However, his German origins were eventually to come back to haunt him. At the same time that the raiders and their prisoners were landing at Emirau, Wilde was incarcerated as an enemy alien in a concentration camp in Australia. Although he was released before the end of the war, his family say that he was a broken man and never fully recovered before his death in 1950. It is ironic that despite his treatment as an enemy alien, he was asked, and he voluntarily gave, valuable information of the coastline around Emirau to

Carl Leopold Bruno Wilde standing next to Juanita Wilde's memorial on Emirau Island

help the American invasion of the island against the Japanese in 1943.

Just after Wilde and Juanita first moved to Emirau in late-1912, another German arrived to help them set out new plantations. John Meehan, in his 1997 tribute to Wilde said that Robert Eyssen, as a young seaman, had brought Juanita to Emirau Island back in 1912. Why or how Eyssen, the son of a Guatemalan coffee plantation owner, was there is not known. On his nineteenth birthday in 1911 he had joined the German Imperial Navy as a midshipman. He was to make a career in the German navy rising eventually to the rank of *Konteradmiral.* Little did this young Eyssen know when he left Emirau in 1913 that he would return nearly thirty years later under very different circumstances.

On the outbreak of war Eyssen was serving on SMS *Karlsruhe*, a brand new light cruiser operating in the Caribbean as a raider, seeking out allied merchant shipping. She sank or captured seventeen merchant ships and had close encounters with British warships. In November 1914 *Karlsruhe* was off Trinidad when an unexplained explosion blew away her bows and she sank, killing 263 of her crew. Eyssen was one of 150 who survived, returning to Germany to continue his naval career.

Although there is no documented foundation to support what follows, there are too many coincidences to disregard a simple theory about why Eyssen was in the area in 1912 or 1913. There are no immigration or port records showing any Eyssen entering the region in the pre-war period as a civilian so he was possibly on naval duty as part of the administration of German New Guinea. At this time a beautiful Government motor sloop called the SMS *Komet* was used around New Guinea which, on the outbreak of war in 1914, was captured in a remote bay in the Bismarck Archipelago in a somewhat spectacular way. Clearly, Eyssen was not on board because he would have been captured and interned but it is possible that he had some connection with the sloop or had previously been a junior officer on her. We know from later events that he always bemoaned the loss of German territories and possessions in the South Pacific as a result of the Treaty of Versailles. He was to take serious revenge on the island of Nauru which he said had been stolen by the British. It is also known from Eyssen's war diary that in 1940 he personally changed the name of his new raider from *Ems* to *Komet*, perhaps knowing that he was to return to the South Pacific. We will never know whether rekindling the *Komet* name was part of his retribution plan, but fate clearly resulted in three German ships and hundreds of prisoners under Eyssen's command arriving on Emirau in late-1940.

SMS Komet used by the Government Administrator in German New Guinea prior to WW1

The answer to the question of why Eyssen chose Emirau to release his captives is now reasonably obvious: he knew the island from when he was a youngster; he would have known the anchorages and maybe he knew of the memorial to Juanita, whom he had known. He is also reported to have told some survivors that he wanted to release them on an island under British control where he knew there would be plenty of food and water and a reasonable chance of quick release.

At the time of the outbreak of WWII the plantation was managed by Charles Cook and his wife. Another couple, Trevor and Olga Collett were Seventh Day Adventists who operated a small saw mill on the other side of the island from the Cooks. Great consternation was raised among the local inhabitants when a ship appeared on the shores of Emirau on the evening of Friday 20 December and there was panic when the sea-plane carried out scouting sorties over the island. Cook told his boss boy to make sure that the ship was watched and told another to run and warn the Colletts. Cook assumed that it had arrived for fresh water and provisions and would only stay for a short time. He decided that he and his wife should hide until the ship had gone, asking his native boys to look after his wife should anything happen to him. Later that evening the ship disappeared and all thought that the excitement was over. Early next morning panic set in again as the three raiders appeared and anchored off the south-east tip of Emirau. Word came to Cook that a substantial number of armed Germans were being ferried ashore at Cook's wharf near Eulolou village. The Cooks had a small lorry, the only motorised transport on the island, and Charles Cook drove his wife from the Homestead to find the Colletts and to decide with them what to do. In the confusion, Cook and his wife came face to face with a platoon of armed Germans from the first landing party. The leading officer advanced on Cook with a handshake and declared rather formally that the island was to be requisitioned in the name of the Third Reich and enquired about facilities to accommodate and feed a large number of captives.

Cook reached the landing point and told a German officer that they were unable to make contact with the outside world because their only motor launch was currently in Rabaul and that the regular supply boat had visited the island in the previous week. In reality, their launch was on neighbouring Mussau Island and the supply boat was due any day. The officer seemed satisfied that there was no immediate risk of anybody escaping the island and warning the authorities.

The Germans started landing those prisoners chosen to be released, giving priority to the women, children and wounded. Motor launches ferried a total of 496 survivors to the island together with a plentiful supply of drinking water, black bread, rice, and basic medical supplies. The Germans had two other objectives: to find and destroy any radio equipment on the island

and to kill five working bullocks for meat. Two were taken in the lorry back to the raiders; the others were to be butchered for the prisoners.

While the majority of the 496 were to savour their freedom, there were 150 prisoners on *Orion* who would feel dejected: they knew that their ordeal was to continue. The disagreement between Eyssen and Weyher over the fate of their captives had continued. Eyssen wanted to release everybody while Weyher said that only the women, children and non-European prisoners should be released. In the end there was a botched compromise: the majority of those already imprisoned on *Orion* were to stay, together with some of the younger men on *Komet* who had to be transferred to *Orion*. But there were inconsistencies: thirteen of *Rangitane*'s fifteen New Zealand Fleet Air Arm recruits on *Komet* were released despite their age and affiliation yet sixty-four year old James Adams, clearly ill, was detained and was to die on *Orion* within three months. One person who was due to be released was Father Ernest Ball. He was reported as having been a stalwart throughout the previous weeks, administering to those needing spiritual comfort. True to his nature and calling, he volunteered to stay on *Orion* and accompany the prisoners wherever fate would take them.

The German captains obviously wanted to leave as quickly as possible in case the alarm had been raised. In exchange for a gun and a lifeboat with oars, Eyssen accepted Upton's word of honour that the lifeboat would not be used to get help for twenty-four hours, threatening otherwise to destroy the wireless station at Kavieng. Eyssen made an undertaking not to attack any ship sent to rescue them and asked Upton to broadcast a message when everybody had been rescued, saying that he would sleep better knowing that everybody was safe. Eyssen also told Upton not to bother sending the message in code because the raiders now had the code books.

The injured, women, children and older survivors were ferried by Cook in his truck the eight miles to the Homestead, initially under armed guard. The majority of able-bodied survivors started to walk in the mid-day heat. Many survivors had few clothes and many had no footwear. After weeks of incarceration in the ships' holds with little exercise, the survivors had great difficulty in walking while others were to gorge themselves on coconuts and local fruits with inevitable after-effects. Most of the men sported unkempt beards and long hair and must have been as much an unusual sight to the local natives, as the natives were to them. Tug Wilson remarked that the local inhabitants rose to the occasion – they accompanied groups of survivors, offering them coconut milk to offset the ravages of the tropical sun and generally helped to carry baggage and equipment. This was in stark contrast to the story told by Judge and Mrs. Stuart. In an account published in 1967, Mrs. Stuart claimed that the Germans had left the prisoners on Emirau with the intention that they should perish at the hands of cannibals known to populate the island. She further claimed that she and her husband, alone, ventured into the jungle to befriend the cannibals and found that a missionary had recently converted the local people to Christianity. Clearly the passage of time had clouded Mrs. Stuart's memory: the reality was that they were driven in Cook's truck directly to the Homestead where they started making demands to be treated according their perceived higher status. Margaret Osborne recalls that they were treated with the contempt they deserved. A similar distorted account of life on Emirau came from the Pacific Union Recorder, the Seventh Day Adventist magazine. It said that three years before the survivors landed, a missionary counted 300 men, women and children '...covered with revolting skin disease ... eating grubs from decaying timber ... living with pigs under one roof ... and being wholly without God in the world.' The reality was that the Cook and Collett families had operated copra and timber businesses for a number of years and Collett himself maintained the missionary station on the island.

The only survivors who did not make the trek to the Homestead were the non-European crew, described in contemporary reports as native or coloured crew. The majority were Chinese and Filipino from the ships sunk around Nauru and some Tongans and Noumeans from *Notou* captured by *Orion* in August. They had to make their own camp close to where they had landed at Cook's wharf and were kept separate from the remainder of the survivors for the whole of their journey home.

Geoffrey Barley recorded the fact that the relationship between the Germans and their captives changed completely during the final hours. Many of the raiders' crew were given shore leave and gathered coconuts and fruit. They even used *Orion*'s plane to drop explosives in the water to kill fish for the survivors and themselves. Some took photographs of the island, the survivors and the local natives. Another crew member set up an artist's easel and painted a local village scene. There was much banter between captor and ex-captive and philosophising about the futility of war.

Rangitane's butchers prepare a feast

When the last prisoners had been ferried ashore, Eyssen and his fellow officers had a duty to perform: they drove to the monument dedicated to Juanita Wilde to hold a short service of remembrance. Finally, with some degree of theatricality, they formally handed Emirau back to Captain Upton as the representative of the British government, who then made great ceremony of handing it back to Cook. The three German vessels departed at full speed to distance themselves from the island. Eyssen knew that the area would shortly be teeming with ships and aircraft searching for them.

The arrival of nearly 500 people quickly woke up the sleepy island of Emirau and clearly the logistics of feeding and accommodation were to become a challenge. Most of the survivors thought that they were in seventh heaven after the deprivations of living in the ships' holds. They were fortunate: Charles Cook had 175 cattle, fruit was plentiful and Cook's Kanakan workforce was willing to donate vegetables from their smallholdings. Potable water was available and there were medicines and medical facilities available. The women were able to sleep in relative comfort in the bungalows while each ship's company made their own sleeping arrangements either in copra sheds or makeshift camps around the island.

The majority of the survivors were more than happy to join in a communal effort to gather food and firewood and to prepare a huge beef stew in a steel drum. But the Stuarts reverted to type, expecting others to provide for them. *Holmwood*'s Captain Miller said that they made a real nuisance of themselves, demanding a separate hut because 'they did not want anything to do with the rabble.' Miller said of Stuart 'He made unreasonable demands upon his fellow prisoners for the continued maintenance of certain prestige and pre-eminence which were suitable to his office in civilised life, but difficult to keep up on a desert island.'

Monday 23 December dawned and the island's launch, the MV *Malangi,* returned from Mussau and was prepared for the journey to Kavieng. Upton convened a meeting of the captains of the sunken ships and decided that *Rangitane*'s chief officer Hopkins, wireless operator Hallett, boatswain Barker and *Vinni*'s chief officer Jensen would make the journey to break the news to the world that the survivors were safe. Upton would stay on Emirau as overall commanding officer. The seventy mile journey which was navigated by Charles Cook was not easy in a twenty-four foot launch at night but they arrived at Kavieng wharf in the early hours of the Christmas Eve, 1940.

Chapter 9

The rescue

Kavieng had been on alert for many months. Unknown aircraft had been circling the region for some time, thought probably to be from the Japanese base at Truk Lagoon only 600 miles to the north. Ted Bishton, the Amalgamated Wireless Australia (AWA) operator was getting out of bed when Phil Jones, the manager of the local Burns Philip store, contacted him to say a small launch had just arrived with some strange passengers. Bishton's first impressions were that they were Germans, particularly the Norwegian Jensen, from *Vinni,* 'who had a suspiciously foreign accent and insisted on clicking his heels.' District Officer John Merrylees instructed Bishton to raise Rabaul on the radio in code to say that 500 men, women and children were on Emirau and were in urgent need of medical supplies and food. *Rangitane's* First Officer Hopkins disagreed, saying that the normal mercantile codes had been compromised; this was the first intimation to the outside world that security may have been breached by the German raiders. Merrylees suggested using the Slater Telegraphy Code used by local shipping to maintain commercial secrecy, but Hopkins again objected saying that Eyssen may be suspicious of a message he could not decypher and might carry out his threat to destroy the wireless station. Hopkins also said that a plain language message would get to Eyssen faster to let him know that his ex-prisoners had managed to make contact with civilisation. Bishton was told to get ready to move the wireless equipment at a moment's notice if there was any sign of enemy attack.

Ted Bishton sent the message and Harry Holland, the AWA operator in Rabaul, replied two hours later, cheekily suggesting that 'Kavieng must have started their Christmas festivities a little too early.' After being told in no uncertain terms that this was a real emergency, the wheels of government started turning and the story was about to explode on the world.

In his later report to the Australian government, Merrylees said that he was extremely suspicious when the party of bedraggled officers first set foot in Kavieng. He said that he interrogated them carefully, asking questions about various shipping companies and their knowledge of Australia and New Zealand. He seemed to be quite happy with the fact that Barker, who was claiming to be a boatswain, must be genuine because he '... looked the petty officer type.' Merrylees's greatest concern was that the survivors had learned that the raiders were returning to destroy the phosphate processing installations on the island of Nauru over 1000 miles away and that the islanders must be warned.

This was to be the most unusual Christmas Eve in Kavieng as Merrylees set a rescue operation in motion. The 400 ton government schooner *Leander* was already in Kavieng and supply, medical and billeting officers were appointed to provision her. An air force flying boat arrived from Rabaul carrying the regional Administrator Sir Walter McNicol and a naval intelligence officer, Hugh Mackenzie, who immediately interviewed Hopkins and his colleagues. *Leander* finally set sail for Emirau in the late morning and another smaller boat, *Shamrock*, owned by a local businessman, was provisioned and set off in the afternoon. McNicol arranged for the requisitioning of SS *Nellore*, a 6,800 ton passenger cargo vessel, instructing it to sail immediately from Rabaul to Kavieng and to make preparations to take all the survivors to Townsville on the Australian mainland. Eyssen on *Komet* was able to decypher these coded instructions and learnt that help was on the way a long time before his ex-captives knew.

Conscious of the fact that word of the survivors would soon spread through the town, arrangements were made to censor all post leaving Kavieng from Friday 27 December. The local censor, Mr. Burne, reported that the mail was slightly heavier than normal and there had been few references to the events of the last few days.

Back on Emirau the survivors were in their third day of freedom. Many were able to sleep in copra sheds, many made their own shelters and wigwams fashioned from tree branches and palm leaves. There had been several tropical downpours and accommodation was swamped, but nobody really grumbled. Although anything was better than being imprisoned below the water line in an enemy ship, the women said that at least on the ships they did not have any rats.

Al fresco dining

The women and ships' cooks established a routine for feeding everybody with basic provisions and the food was described as divine compared with the food in captivity. The beautiful beaches and crystal clear waters of the sea were an attraction to anybody who could throw modesty to the wind. The only real problems arose from insect bites and skin abrasions from the poisonous coral reefs, but *Rangitane*'s Dr. Crawford and some of the CORB ladies were always on hand to provide treatment.

To help give a focus, it was decided that Father Kelly would conduct a midnight mass on Christmas Eve. The women who had formed a choir group on *Kulmerland* got together and practised some hymns, making up the words whenever they couldn't remember the correct ones. Some of *Batory*'s Polish women managed to acquire sufficient materials to make the vestments, and a surprisingly impressive altar was built on the beach.

Just as the final preparations were being made for the service, lights appeared out at sea. A Morse lamp signalled that it was *Leander* and that she had medical supplies, a doctor, food and, most importantly, cigarettes. The New Zealand survivors immediately assumed that it was their navy's 8,500 ton light cruiser HMNZS *Leander* and were a little disappointed that it was only a local schooner with the same name. Signals were exchanged and it was agreed that the schooner would sail to Eulolou Harbour at the eastern end of the island and tie up at Cook's wharf.

Midnight mass on Emirau has been described with great emotion in many personal accounts. The combination of relief that the world knew of their plight, and personal gratitude that they had come through relatively unscathed added great poignancy to the service. Nearly everybody came, either to take part or to watch, including hundreds of local inhabitants. The more seriously wounded were carried close to the altar. The service started when the choir walked in procession out of the trees towards the altar singing 'All come all ye Faithful' and 'Hark the Herald Angels Sing.' Betsy Sandbach and Geraldine Edge said 'The light of the lanterns lit up the solemn faces of the men and women brought together by a common impulse, to give thanks for their deliverance and to pray for their less fortunate companions.' Finally, the National Anthem was sung with such conviction, everybody wanting it to be their parting shot of defiance against their enemy. But there were some people missing from the service: Captain Upton and some of the other ships' captains drove with Cook to Eulolou to meet *Leander*'s officers. Upton had received a report that a large fire had been seen earlier in the day at the southern end of Mussau Island, just 15 miles away and was worried that it may have been a distress signal from other ships' survivors. At daybreak *Leander* sailed to Mussau and the local natives confirmed that they had seen no ships recently nor were there any Europeans present on the island.

On Christmas Day morning the schooner *Leander* anchored just off the jetty at the Homestead and delivered the first provisions by pinnace. Apart from the cigarettes, everybody was hoping for ingredients for a traditional Christmas Dinner. They were to be disappointed. It took all morning for the sick and wounded to be transferred to the schooner followed by the families, including husbands. When Judge Stuart heard that a flying boat was on its way, he insisted that he and his wife had priority on it because he urgently needed to report major breaches of security known only to him. He wrote a letter to Captain Upton:

> 23 December 1940
>
> Dear Captain Upton,
>
> I hardly need to stress the fact that after the wounded my wife and I are the most urgent persons involved from the point of view of getting on to where I can cable in safe code.
>
> If as a result of the strong steps you are taking to get into touch with the outside world a 32 seater is sent over, please do not fail to expedite my claim to prompt forward transport with priority over all but the seriously wounded and non-convalescents.
>
> May I put in writing my appreciation of your tenacity and determination when your ship was attacked, also of the great tact you must have displayed in obtaining so many releases from the Germans, also for the excellence of your arrangements here, despite serious difficulties.
>
> Wm Stuart, Chief Justice of Tonga on leave then
> Judge Chambers, Georgetown, British Guiana

The Stuarts' demands were rejected: they had to make do with a cramped deck on *Leander* with everybody else. The little boat *Shamrock* arrived and loaded the Chinese and Filipino crew from the other end of the island at Cook's wharf.

On Christmas Day in Kavieng, Mackenzie and Squadron Leader Preston left by flying boat for Emirau and *Nellore* arrived in Kavieng from Rabaul but stayed tentatively offshore. She had no navigation charts for the approach channel and signalled a request for an experienced pilot to escort her. The only qualified pilot was Les Bell who had gone to Rabaul. Qualifications were thrown to the wind in the emergency: Colin Mackellar had experience of navigating smaller boats into Kavieng and was taken by Merrylees in the station's pinnace to board and direct *Nellore* to anchor between Kavieng and Nag Island. In the evening *Leander* appeared with the first consignment of about eighty cramped survivors consisting of all the women, children and wounded together with husbands and other men. When they rounded Nag they could not believe their eyes – *Nellore* was anchored with all lights ablaze and crew waiting for them in their crisp whites. Betsy Sandbach and Geraldine Edge could not believe it: 'Oh, the joy of being on a British ship once more!' By midnight everybody was tucked up in the first proper bed for a month. At the same time, and in very sharp contrast, *Shamrock* arrived back from Emirau with 101 Chinese and Filipinos. They were ushered ashore into Kavieng's native compound for the night.

Survivors being towed in lifeboats to Nellore

Nellore set off for Emirau to embark the remaining 316 survivors on Boxing Day morning with Colin Mackellar acting as pilot again. He stayed on board to help negotiate the waters around Emirau, for which services he was later to submit an invoice for the princely sum of £75. The government refused to pay such a high sum and Mackellar threatened legal action. It took nearly a year for the two sides to settle on a £25 pilotage fee. Charles Cook had wanted to lift his motor launch *Malangi* onto *Nellore* so it could help ferry the survivors from Emirau. Unfortunately the davits were not strong enough and he had to sail her eighty miles back to the island. Those who were already on *Nellore* were delighted when they saw their friends waiting on the beach when they arrived at Emirau. It was taking too long to transfer everybody in the small launch so *Nellore*'s lifeboats were used as mules and towed behind a launch. Most of the cabins on board had been assigned to the injured and families, so the decks and public areas were covered by very happy men just glad to be on their way home. Tug Wilson commented about how many had taken souvenirs from Emirau on board. There are many reports about how well the crew coped with their new charges. *Nellore* was not a large ship and had modest catering facilities, so every mealtime was provided in five sittings; no sooner had the last diners finished lunch, the first sitting for dinner was to start.

Happy faces on Nellore

Early next morning *Nellore* sailed into Rabaul to an amazing welcome: the 300 local inhabitants had made a collection of old clothes, footwear and provisions for the survivors, all of which were delivered to the ship. The women, in particular, were delighted to dress in more ladylike attire while the men were quite happy to exchange their dirty ripped shorts for baggy Edwardian plus-fours and knotted handkerchiefs for bowler hats. Tug Wilson parodied Churchill by saying that he was 'amazed that so much had been collected by so few for so many.' Betsy Sandbach and Geraldine Edge commented that Mrs. Stuart was always the first in the queue and that 'her pushing powers exceeded her stature.' They also commented that she never failed to compete over the spoils, despite her scorn for the rabble, and that Father Kelly had to be summoned to act as a referee. The women made a special effort to dress smartly for their first dinner on board.

Nellore gained a number of additional passengers recruited to record exactly who had survived, who had been killed and who was still on *Orion* and presumably on their way to Germany. There were also intelligence officers who needed to start documenting the many stories and theories leading to alleged breaches of security, everything from the fanciful to the farcical. *Nellore* finally left in the afternoon and everybody settled down for what they hoped would be an uneventful journey to Townsville. Luckily, they had no reason to worry. Some men took the opportunity to shave off their beards and get a decent haircut. Everybody knew that they would be in front of the world's press when they arrived and they wanted to look their best.

The only ship's captain on *Nellore* was Upton, who took overall responsibility for the survivors. The remainder had arrived in Rabaul by flying boat and had gone on to the Navy Office at Port Moresby. Although arriving late at night, the captains were interrogated until the early hours of the following morning and then throughout the morning. They left by air for Melbourne via Townsville and Brisbane where debriefing continued until the afternoon of Saturday 28 December. Upton would be interrogated separately when aboard *Nellore*.

The debriefing covered every aspect which would be of immediate use to defensive forces. This covered the description, characteristic markings, speed, armaments etc. of each raider. It covered the exact sequence of events leading to the capture of each ship, particularly the use of *Rangitane*'s radio prior to her interception and the many issues of breach of security. Upton and the other captains clearly had spent many long hours when in captivity discussing the events of the last four weeks and they presented a consensus view that security had been seriously compromised. In his formal report, Upton's list included concerns about merchant codes falling into the Germans' hands; the fact that some *Holmwood* captives had been told by the Germans that the *Rangitane* would be captured the following day, (and it was); that the three raiders had been waiting exactly on *Rangitane*'s track; that they knew that Upton had not followed his instructed course on his outward passage; they knew where *Rangitata* was going to be, and so on. There were general comments about press indiscretions which made sailing times and destinations easily determined; about lax security in wireless traffic, and the fact that the Germans must have an established regional base, probably in the Caroline islands.

Just before leaving Emirau, Captains Eyssen, Weyher and Pshunder agreed that the raider flotilla would split up. *Kulmerland* was to return to Japan to replenish supplies and *Orion*, with her 150 prisoners, would head for Lamotrek Atoll where she would be re-supplied by the tanker *Ole Jacob*. Eyssen had unfinished business and wanted to take *Komet* back to Nauru to destroy the phosphate plant. His plan was to sail via Rabaul and to use his speedboat *Meteorit* to mine the approaches to the town. He was irritated that the speedboat was again out of action and may have again regretted sinking *Holmwood,* which would have been a perfect auxiliary minelayer.

Komet set out on the 1000 mile return journey to Nauru. Captain Weyher referred to Nauru as Eyssen's pet project. It had been his intended destination on 27 November before they encountered *Holmwood* and had been the island originally chosen for offloading the prisoners. Eyssen was now intent on getting there and exacting some revenge.

Phosphate mining had become the only industry on Nauru and was owned jointly by the British, Australian and New Zealand governments. The phosphate company had made a major investment in phosphate mining, storage and handling equipment including a ship loading cantilever and a fleet of ships designed especially for the phosphate trade. Three of the company's ships, *Triona, Triadic* and *Triaster* had already been sunk by Eyssen's raiders during their last visit earlier in December; it was now Eyssen's intention to destroy the loading facilities and oil depots to stop the export of phosphate and to destroy the radio facility.

Komet arrived off Nauru before daybreak on 27 December and Eyssen signalled by Morse lamp his intention and that everybody should be evacuated out of range by a specified time. He warned that he would immediately destroy the civic area if any attempt was made to use the radio. Bill Bott, Nauru's phosphate manager, immediately evacuated the area, sending the women, children and less able men into the underground conveyor belt tunnels. When it was daylight, the assistant harbour master, the only person who knew semaphore, was told by Bott to stall for time while the radio equipment was quickly dismantled and moved away from danger. Part of the semaphore exchange was a compliment paid by Eyssen to Nauru's artists: apparently Tom Cude, the Nauru chief of police, had persuaded the phosphate company to camouflage the massive oil tanks with paintings of thatched huts, palm trees and blue sky. But this did not fool Eyssen: at the appointed time, more than 200 shells were fired, completely destroying the phosphate infrastructure. Thankfully nobody was killed or injured. It was amazing that nobody had been warned on Nauru that a raider was on its way, despite the information having been given by the captains released in Kavieng on Christmas Eve. There was much speculation and intrigue about why there was no forewarning. Investigations ran in parallel with the ongoing investigation into leakage of information on the phosphate company's ships sunk earlier in December.

Nauru wireless made its first emergency report of the shelling saying that the aggressor was named *Manyo Maru* and displayed Japanese flags during the attack. This infuriated the authorities and the Foreign Office in London immediately instructed its ambassador in Tokyo to demand an explanation. Similarly the Australian government made strong representations to the Japanese Consular-General in Sydney. Unfortunately, the first report had to be retracted when witnesses on Nauru agreed that the Japanese markings had been covered by swastikas when the attack was actually made. This did little to appease the outrage, especially when Japan appeared to drag its feet in responding to the protests. The spat between the governments rumbled for months; it quickly became clear to the Allies that raiders were being re-provisioned from supply ships which themselves had been re-supplied in Japan, an officially neutral country. The arguments were a prelude to what would happen in the Pacific region one year later.

When Eyssen decided to exact his revenge on Nauru, he probably had not thought through the wider political implications of his actions. It must have been obvious to him that approaching Nauru under the guise of the Japanese flag was going to have political repercussions. He probably had not realised that Japan was also a significant importer of phosphates from Nauru and Ocean islands. One of the unexpected results was that it gave Australia and New Zealand the excuse they needed to place defensive bases on the outlying islands of the mandated territories. Such military installations were prohibited in the aftermath of the Treaty of Versailles, but Eyssen's attack was, in effect, a breach of the treaty and justified arming the islands. It also highlighted the apparent use by Germany of some of Japan's Pacific mandated territories, particularly the Marshall Islands, to re-provision its raiders. Australia made a number of fruitless representations to Japan for the practice to be stopped, but Japan at that time was already planning to escalate the use of the islands for her own military purposes. The most significant new Allied policy would be the monitoring and challenging of any ship sailing under a neutral flag, particularly a Japanese flag. This was to lead to a number of bad-tempered diplomatic exchanges with the Japanese government.

The damage to the equipment on Nauru stopped phosphate export for two months; luckily, the Australian government had the foresight in 1939 to anticipate wartime supply problems and had increased phosphate production and stockpiled reserves on the mainland. The old ship loading methods using baskets and lighters was resurrected, while the storage silos and loading cantilevers were rebuilt over a four month period. Although export quantities never recovered to their pre-war levels, it must have been heartbreaking for the local staff to have to sabotage all their reconstruction work on 11 December, 1941 knowing that the Japanese were on the point of invading the island.

Chapter 10

Allegations and censorship

Back on *Nellore* it was obvious that while the highly contentious allegations coming from the survivors could be contained and controlled within the Naval Board, the same could not be said when the media would eventually get access to them. There were potentially hundreds of people wanting to tell their own story to the waiting world. Censorship was essential and the procedure was already established. Australia's Department of Information had been set up at the beginning of the war to control government publicity and censorship. This was to prevent sensitive information reaching the enemy, to prevent false impressions of Australia being portrayed abroad and to maintain high morale at home. Its minister, Senator Foll, had been in the job only for a few weeks and this was to be his baptism of fire. He placed a complete censorship blanket on the press and radio as soon as the release of the prisoners from Emirau was made known to the security services.

Censorship staff were immediately despatched to Townsville to meet the survivors on *Nellore*, with strict instructions about what could and could not be published. Meanwhile, the Australian and New Zealand governments agreed the first press release which described only the release of the survivors and named Emirau as the island. No details were given of which ships had been involved until a full list of survivors and those detained on *Orion* had been finalised. They further agreed the censorship guidelines for the next few days: no photographs and no reference to the existence of photographs of the raiders; no reference to numbers, descriptions, procedures, routes or likely base used by the raiders, and no mention of the name of the rescue ship nor the port she was heading for. It was at this point that the system started collapsing. The Minister for Air, Jack McEwen, decided to publicise immediately the part played by the

Royal Australian Air Force in the rescue of the senior ships' officers, releasing details of the first interviews to the press. Commander Long, the director of naval intelligence, was angry, as was William Hughes, the navy minister. But the press loved the story and it was to become a feeding frenzy over the following weeks.

On New Year's Eve the Department of Information issued its first press statement announcing the rescue of the 496 prisoners and all the ships involved, making specific reference to *Turakina*'s attempt at resistance to capture. The statement was clearly aimed as a patriotic snub to the German raiders. Also confirmed were the names of some of the CORB escorts who had been killed and the fact that a number of other crew from the ships had been killed. The press had few facts to report but editors still managed to fill pages with detailed descriptions, many incorrect, of Emirau. The press would have to wait for the detailed stories until *Nellore* reached the safety of Townsville.

As the authorities in Townsville were preparing for the arrival of their unplanned guests, there was a major influx of officials and representatives from other parts of the country. A plane arrived carrying a government Under-Secretary representing the Premier, three officers from the Naval Office, the Deputy Director of the Department of Information and the State Censor. Also on board were representatives of all the companies whose ships had been sunk, two selected representatives of the national press and a senior officer from the Commonwealth Investigation Branch (CIB) to manage the country's security interests. This was clearly a huge event as far as the authorities were concerned and it was planned like a military operation. The immigration authorities had to deal with 496 persons with no passports, the health department had to apply Australia's strict quarantine regulations and medical staff knew that there were many casualties requiring treatment and convalescence. Extra clerks were needed to handle free telegrams to next-of-kin, and the cost was charged to the Prime Minister's department. Then, of course, there was the question of how to interview those who wanted to give information to the authorities and how to guard the rescue ship and to control access by the eager press corps.

The most demanding question was how to accommodate, feed and disperse everybody to their individual destinations. It was decided that the government would charter a special train to take the survivors from Townsville to Sydney, from where they would be dispersed. The Queensland Tourist Bureau were given the job of organising trains with the correct number of sleeper carriages for the injured, women and children, and arrangements were made for meals to be available at regular stops on the 1200 mile journey. The Red Cross and the Australian Comforts Fund organised for everybody to receive a bag of comforts at the start of the journey – soap, toothbrushes and toothpaste, cosmetics, tobacco and confectionary.

The world had been told that the survivors would land at Townsville on New Year's Day. *Nellore* had been expected to arrive at Townsville in the morning but uncertainty set in when there was no sign of her. Being under wartime radio silence regulations, there was no indication of where she might be. Senator Harry Foll, the Minister for Information, was anxious that relatives waiting for news would worry that the rescue ship had suffered a mis-hap and instructed the senior CIB officer to ask the local air force to help: they despatched two Wirraway training planes to locate the ship but they had only limited range and returned with no news. There was some misunderstanding: the CIB asked for permission for *Nellore* to break radio silence and to give her position, but this permission was never relayed to the local officers to implement.

After many tense hours, *Nellore* finally arrived at 10.30 p.m. and anchored eight miles offshore to maintain a quarantine zone. The survivors now felt they had reached a truly safe haven. When he heard of the safe arrival, Senator Foll asked that the press should be allowed immediate access in order that the first stories could appear in the following morning's papers to allay relatives' fears. The Quarantine Authority were unhappy with this but acceded to the suggestion that escorted reporters could visit the ship by launch and conduct first interviews from the launch by shouting to anybody on deck. It was after midnight when the launch arrived at Nellore's side to find that there was only one passenger who begrudgingly and suspiciously answered questions about the treatment of the captives. After only five minutes the interviewee disappeared leaving the journalists with meagre material. But anything was better than nothing: the newspapers would be able to confirm the safe arrival of the rescue ship and could print the first of many human interest stories. The launch started the eight mile return to Townsville with the journalists typing their reports by the light of hurricane lamps, getting approval from the local censor who had accompanied them. The journalists narrowly beat the press deadline in Brisbane and Sydney newspapers and the first stories were syndicated around the world.

Incorrect assertion that there were children on board Rangitane

The full force of officialdom boarded *Nellore* next day. Immigration, customs and quarantine officers had their moments of glory. The newspaper reporters were given access to the passengers when the Quarantine Authority was finally satisfied. Then the stories tumbled out from anybody who would stand still long enough for reporters to ask their questions. The whole sorry saga was repeated many times and tales of hardship were pounced on by the press. The local evening newspapers were the first to publish the stories, followed by the national regional morning papers. Although the censor had to approve every story to ensure that national security was not compromised further, the headlines were dramatic: 'Children shelled...', 'Nazi atrocities...', 'Vile conditions...', 'Dastardly attack...' The same stories were told, embellished and retold. The stories reached London and the British national press followed suit.

Conditions On Prison Ships Worse Than Those On Altmark

CAPTIVES' STORIES OF CALLOUS TREATMENT BY GERMAN COMMANDERS

Conditions in which the captives, including women, were held on board the Pacific raiders were worse than what they had heard of the hell-ship Altmark, said survivors when they arrived in a rescue vessel at an Australian port.

The food was described as abominable, machine guns were trained down the hatches in one ship, washing and sanitary arrangements were disgusting. In another ship 15 women were kept for three days in a small room below the galley and were allowed on deck only once—to see the burial service for a woman victim of the raider's shelling.

Typical newspaper report

There were many stories about how badly the Germans treated the captives. This irritated a number of people: Molly Black and Flora McDonald were very annoyed and made a formal complaint to the censor about press exaggeration. While they said that stories about ill-treatment were totally untrue, they were most concerned that the raider captains would hear about the allegations and persecute their remaining captives. Tug Wilson said that many of the stories were over-dramatised nonsense. But the chief censor had his own problems. He had received a flurry of complaints from his regional staff and the editors of some of the southern newspapers because of contradictory application of censorship rules. The Port Moresby censor had cleared information which the Papuan Courier then published, but the Melbourne and Sydney censors had refused the printing of the very same stories. Stories syndicated abroad started to return to the Australian press, modified and embellished into apparently new stories. In particular, a story in the Hong Kong newspapers named Captain Miller and the *Holmwood*, information which had been specifically banned. The Sydney Daily and Sunday Telegraph were frustrated that they had had stories spiked which named ships and captains, yet the Melbourne Argus appeared to be freely publishing the very same material.

The Department of Information finally released a complete list of those who had died or had been rescued from Emirau and those believed to be still captive on the raiders. But this carefully compiled list was to be a problem: it included some serious errors as twelve crewmen from *Triaster* were listed as survivors but they were in fact still prisoners on *Orion*. Some others named as survivors were actually the names of the next-of-kin of survivors. The Department of Information had to place a grovelling apology in the press, putting the blame on typographical errors and '...telegraphic mutilations.' The Melbourne *Argus* published a stinging leader article about ministerial bungling and inter-departmental rivalries. It made a searing attack on Senator Foll who, only a week previously, had promised the nation that he would take a greater personal control over censorship and the release of information to the public. The *Argus* said that some of the bungling 'appears to have been due to petty rivalry between two branches of the services for whatever credit attaches to the rescue of victims of raiders which the Air Force cannot locate and the Navy cannot run down.' Senator Foll was told by the paper to 'gain control and refuse to allow his senior colleagues in the Cabinet who happen to be service ministers to interfere with his censorship duties.' The *Argus* leader led to a firestorm of criticism and personal attacks which divided the security service, censors, armed forces ministers and the press. The Navy Office bore the brunt: they were to have absolutely nothing to do with the press in the future and all dealings had to be routed through the Department of Information.

The censors still had to suppress information which they thought to be prejudicial to security, particularly the extent of knowledge about the appearance and armament of the raiders and their tactics in changing appearance. But access to so many survivors could no longer be controlled effectively and more and more stories about security lapses appeared in the headlines. The most damaging concerned the widespread belief among survivors that the raiders knew exactly when and where to find *Rangitane* and that there must have been security breaches in New Zealand. The press went as far as saying that the Australian authorities were going to take action and that blame lay with New Zealand. This infuriated the New Zealand Government and a secret cable from the Prime Minister was sent to the Australian Prime Minister which, even by the standards of diplomatic protocol, was blunt. The Commonwealth of Australia was firmly advised in a cable not to interfere, that the issues would be investigated from Wellington and that the Dominion of New Zealand would take whatever action it thought fit.

Reference was made to an article in which *Rangitane*'s quartermaster Ted Phillips said that there was leakage of information in New Zealand. He said that as well as knowing the route of *Rangitane*, the Germans knew the movements of another liner. Phillips went on to say that much information was known to the raiders 'that would not be known to the ordinary man in the street.' Another unnamed source in the article said that raiders were getting precise information on shipping positions. But what really irked New Zealand was a quote 'from an un-named high judicial officer' that the Germans knew the exact contents of *Holmwood*'s cargo when it left the Chatham Islands and that he had other knowledge so serious that 'it would lead to imminent arrests in New Zealand.' The high judicial officer was, of course, the passenger Judge Stuart who also claimed that his wife, who was apparently fluent in German, overheard a number of conversations which gave evidence of culpability. Stuart also claimed that he 'had already recommended the arrest of certain persons as Fifth Columnists but the authorities chose to do nothing about it.' The New Zealand government took the unusual step of stating in a press release that the un-named judicial officer categorically was not from New Zealand. Unfortunately many of Stuart's allegations gained credence by being supported by Captain Upton who, with his fellow officers, was beginning to repeat the stories to the press. The most damaging was that immediately after *Holmwood*'s capture, her captain had been told by the Germans that they would be 'capturing a big ship next day.' *Rangitane* was indeed captured the following day, apparently proving everybody's suspicions.

The Australian Prime Minister replied to New Zealand expressing regret at how the stories had reached the press and the apparent failure of censorship. He tried to provide explanations for some of the allegations but it was clear that a major investigation was needed to allay the public astonishment at events.

The authorities finally cleared *Nellore* to move to berth on the Townsville wharf. Every ship in the harbour sounded their sirens and hundreds of workers and townspeople lined the shore waving and shouting their welcome. Medical staff immediately set about assessing the condition of the survivors and the Red Cross and Australian Comforts Fund volunteers attended to everybody's immediate needs. Women came on board offering free chocolates, cigarettes and gum. Despite the meticulous planning, the most urgent requirements were for things that nobody had thought about: opticians were summoned to replace spectacles and dentists to try to replace lost dentures. The medical team spent a long time with the more seriously injured, particularly Florence Mundie who had lost an arm. The fact that the German doctor on *Kulmerland* had handed over all of her treatment notes when she was landed at Emirau did not go unnoticed. Florence later praised the treatment she had received from friend and foe alike. The CORB escorts were delighted to find that their representative Mr. Garnett had flown up from Sydney to greet them. While he was delighted to see the escorts, there was obviously deep regret over those who had died on *Rangitane*. But he had equally bad news to tell: eight of their original CORB colleagues from *Batory* had begun their return trip to England on the SS *Port Wellington* but contact had been lost and the ship was weeks overdue and presumed lost. Garnett was not to know that another successful raider, *Pinguin,* had sunk *Port Wellington* and all of the CORB staff had been taken prisoner on the raider and would eventually arrive in POW camps in Germany.

Only the European passengers were allowed to disembark to experience what would become persistent cheering and flag-waving over the following days. The Chinese and Filipino survivors were again to be kept separate. The women survivors were the first to descend the gangway into a long low shed and were presented with a choice of dozens of new dresses and outfits of all sizes and colours. They were even given suitcases to carry their new clothes and the mementoes of their time on Emirau. Everybody was allowed a few hours to wander around Townsville but few had expected the constant attention that they would attract. Geoffrey Barley said that everywhere they went they were molested by autograph hunters and reporters. He found peace and quiet by returning to his cabin on the ship. Everybody had to be back on board *Nellore* for a final roll call and an early dinner before being escorted the short distance to the railway station for their journey to Sydney.

Women survivors in their new clothes

Chapter 11

The journey home

It had been decided that the majority of the non-European survivors would be repatriated from Townsville, instead of travelling to Sydney. The Noumean and Tongan crew survivors, being classified as residents within the Australian commonwealth area, would also travel to Sydney. The first train took the European survivors except Thomas Smith who travelled in the second train. Smith was one of the *Baltannic* crew to be repatriated on *Rangitane*. It is not recorded why he was on the second train but it may have been decided that he should not travel with some of the Polish survivors on the first train with whom he had had a continuing disagreement. Smith had made a formal report to the intelligence service, saying that when they first boarded *Rangitane* in Auckland, he had been told by *Baltannic*'s captain to keep an eye on a Polish man and woman who were thought to be dangerous. Smith said that he had seen the man, Hieronim Nawraccala, escorted to *Rangitane* under police guard in Auckland. Smith said that the Pole was over-friendly with the captors, gaining privileges not available to anyone else and even conversing in fluent German using anti-British sentiments. On their last day on the raider Smith 'gave him a severe thrashing' and the antipathy continued on Emirau. Nawraccala apparently continued to be objectionable on *Nellore* 'claiming privileges which could not reasonably be expected.'

The first train had three sleeping carriages and good seating carriages on which passengers could lie. The second train for the non-Europeans consisted of just two second class carriages with no sanitary facilities, water supply or comfortable seats. They were supervised by a Townsville policeman responsible for ensuring that they did not abscond. The train was a scheduled local service and the survivors had to share one compartment with other fare-paying passengers. In his report,

Pike, the policeman, said that he had to make strong complaints to get the accommodation for the survivors upgraded at one of the stops.

The first stage of the journey was 700 miles to Brisbane. The trains left in pouring rain on the evening of 2 January 1941 with members of the press in attendance. Tug Wilson and Geoffrey Barley both said that the reporters and cameramen were a nuisance: the exhausted survivors tried to settle down for the long journey but were disturbed by persistent requests for interviews and photographs. Next morning, the trains made the first of a number of stops at stations to let passengers have refreshments provided by voluntary groups, all co-ordinated by the train company. The trains stopped briefly at Mackay, Rockhampton and Landsburgh. Wherever the railway passed near a populated area, there were always hundreds of welcoming people who would respond with delight when the drivers blew their steam whistles. Sanbach and Edge said that at one station there was a children's tea party set up with tables decorated with crackers, balloons and flowers. They also said that they were delighted to see that two CORB children whom they had escorted on *Batory* had come to meet them at one station.

After two days the trains arrived on the outskirts of Brisbane. Again, the survivors were amazed at their reception: all the houses adjacent to the railway track had windows crowded with excited people waving. This was only the prelude. Brisbane station had been set up to provide a formal welcome. Barriers were needed to control hundreds of the residents who had turned out to witness the big event and the police had to force a way through the crowds for the survivors.

A makeshift dais had been set up on which local dignitaries sat to provide a degree of formality and gravitas. But then another censorship issue exploded. The survivors were officially greeted by Mr. Ned Hanlon, the acting Premier of Queensland. The local radio station 4BH was allowed to broadcast his welcome speech but on the strict understanding that Hanlon was the only person to speak and that he was instructed on exactly what he was allowed to say and, of most importance, what he could not say. This was an established practice when live broadcasts were involved. Everything went well with Hanlon giving a rousing speech, limited according to his instructions. Unfortunately, at the end of his speech, he offered the microphone to Captain Upton to say a few words in reply on behalf of the survivors. Upton did not have permission from the Censor to speak nor had he been briefed on restrictions. Upton offered his heartfelt thanks to everybody involved in the rescue but, in doing so, named the rescue ship and the port of disembarkation, two facts which had been under strict censorship since the beginning of the rescue operation. Queensland's publicity censor later sent a stinging letter to C. R. Carson, manager station 4BH, saying the studio should have immediately cut Upton off the air ' because of his highly dangerous and censorable statements.' He said that such a serious lapse would have been censored had the newspapers alone tried to file a report, but live transmission over the air was dangerous. In retrospect, there seems to have been little point in not releasing the information because *Nellore* had left Townsville and the passengers were all safe.

After the official welcome, the survivors were escorted to the Canberra Hotel for breakfast and to take advantage of bathrooms and hot water. Cars and coaches were laid on for groups to travel in and around Brisbane. This was to be the first time that the international journalists had access to the survivors. In particular, Pathé News cameramen recorded the occasion with the usual patriotic gusto and the film was shown in cinemas throughout the Allied world. The reception given by the ordinary people of Australia was so enthusiastic that Tug Wilson wondered what the reception would have been like if they had returned home as victors, not victims.

Later in the day the survivors were escorted to a single express train for the final journey to Sydney. The departure was missing one passenger: John O'Brian from *Komata* missed the train on purpose, claiming that he didn't like the publicity, preferring to spend the evening enjoying his notoriety in the local pubs. In a very drunken state he went to the Hotel Canberra in Brisbane and asked for a room. By coincidence, there was already a room reserved by a guest named O'Brian so he was shown to the room and got into bed. The real guest later arrived to find a drunken sailor refusing to vacate the room and the hotel called the police. Next morning O'Brian was escorted to a scheduled service train to continue his journey to Sydney in the company of Thomas Smith and the remainder of the non-European crew.

After leaving Brisbane, other censorship problems arose when it was discovered that a journalist from the Brisbane Courier Mail had bought a spool of film from one of the survivors, allegedly containing photographs of the raiders, and had sent it by air to his editor. This was in defiance of well publicised instructions that all photographs had to be handed over to naval intelligence. A stern telegram to the editor ensured that the photographs were all submitted to the censor. It was also found that one of the New Zealand airmen was carrying a letter from Billy Harden who had not been released at Emirau and was still on one of the raiders. It was to his wife telling her of his fate and ended with some observations: 'It is the leaders of the nations that cause the trouble and we just have to put up with it. I never did like war and I like it less now that I have seen some of the other side.' He went on to say 'We have had some Australian newspapers on board, and they are full of strikes etc. for trivial details, and it just makes all of us on board sick to read of them.' The censor did not like this at all, saying that it was an example of German propaganda at work. Billy Harden's wife never received his letter. Despite the many problems, the state censor's final report noted that everybody co-operated well and, somewhat obsequiously, noted that the acting Premier 'did a difficult job well.'

The train arrived at Sydney station just after mid-day on Sunday 5th January to a rapturous welcome and emotional scenes of families welcoming back their loved-ones. The station had been organised with military precision because it was from here that everybody would disperse to be repatriated. Different zones were cordoned off so that survivors from the different ships could be accounted for and forwarded to accommodation reserved for them throughout the city. But first, there was another official welcome, this time a much grander occasion than that in Brisbane. Lord Gowrie, the Governor General of Australia, and Lady Gowrie shook the hand of every survivor before giving a rousing speech praising the courage and fortitude in the face of adversity. Speeches were then given by Federal Treasurer Arthur Fadden on behalf of the Commonwealth and by Sir Henry Manning on behalf of the New South Wales government. Finally, when Captain Upton was introduced to speak on behalf of the survivors, there was loud cheering for his leadership over the previous weeks which, the press reported, could be heard half a mile away. Upton was deeply moved by the demonstration and the press reported that he responded with a shaking voice:

Lord Gowrie welcoming the survivors to Sydney

> I am again honoured to try and put into words what we survivors feel toward the Government and people of Australia for the wonderful manner in which we have been welcomed to these shores. And once again I have to say that

> words are totally inadequate to express our gratitude. I feel, however, that I cannot allow the occasion to pass without recording our heartfelt thanks at the excellent manner in which this railway journey has been organised and the entirely praiseworthy work of the Red Cross and other patriotic societies. Nothing has been a trouble to them.

Fond farewells were said over tea and sandwiches, and each ship's contingent boarded buses to travel to hotels and guest houses. In total, 352 survivors arrived in Sydney out of the 496 who landed at Emirau. The other 144 were the non-European crew who had been repatriated by sea from Townsville. The immigration authorities had the nightmare of keeping track of everybody after they left the station, most of whom had lost their passports and forms of identification. Each shipping company was made responsible for arranging and paying for the subsistence of its employees and passengers while in Australia and for their onward or homeward passage. Citizens of the British Empire had to apply for emergency replacement passports and could decide where their future lay, a decision heavily influenced by the fact that the majority of the men had signed the parole agreeing not to take up arms against Germany. The legal status of the parole was to tax the minds of many government advisors over the following months.

Most of the ships' passengers managed to find a sponsor for their costs while in Sydney, either from their own government representatives or friends and relatives. It was noted in a report to the Prime Minister's office that the majority were only too pleased to receive financial help. However, there were two notable exceptions: the Stuarts, who did little to endear themselves to their fellow travellers, started making excessive demands for their subsistence. They were initially sent to the Hotel Australia together with some of *Rangitane*'s senior officers, but this was clearly not good enough for their perceived status. They were then moved to Petty's Hotel, one of the most exclusive hotels favoured by ex-patriots. 'Mr. and Mrs. Stuart are very difficult persons and have caused much trouble' said the report, and the United Kingdom High Commissioner in Sydney was asked to take charge of them. Their saviour was Lady Edith Hunter, a prominent Auckland socialite, who travelled by flying boat from Auckland and took them back to New Zealand. Lady Hunter was clearly out of the same mould as Mrs. Stuart: she was wife of the late Sir George Hunter MP and a persistent amateur advocate. She personally conducted her legal claim to overturn her husband's will and to challenge the competence of his executors, a case that had started in 1930 and was still rumbling along in 1941. Unfortunately she was not successful and was to fall upon hard times. The press at the time was amazed at a woman taking on the challenge in a male dominated legal system.

The Stuarts boarded Pan American's Pacific Clipper on 19 January to fly back to Britain via Canton Island and America, eventually arriving for Stuart's appointment as Second Puisne Judge in British Guiana. Elizabeth Wood-Ellem, in her book on Queen Salote of Tonga, remarked that the last thing heard of Stuart was that he punched a man in a cinema queue in Georgetown, British Guiana. The fact that the Stuarts had made such damaging allegations about security and claimed to have proof, was frustrating for the authorities, particularly the panel of the official inquiry set up only a few weeks later in New Zealand. They were not given the opportunity to cross-examine the Stuarts, an occasion which would probably have been quite a spectacle. CORB escort Margaret Osborne believed that she had forewarned the authorities about the credibility of the Stuarts. In a letter to her Mother she wrote:

> Now that we are here and the evidence of slander has been laid before the authorities, the Stuarts are going to get it in the neck and I hope so. They cannot be allowed to go around saying the Government chose the lowest types to send out with the children and calling us little better than prostitutes.

Those were his words. Oh dear, as if we had not had enough trials.

The British survivors were eligible for various cash payments and gifts. The Australian federal government had only recently enacted a new seamen's war damage compensation scheme. This provided a maximum grant of £10 for the loss of personal effects while serving on a British ship lost by enemy action. John Snowden was a *Rangitane* plumber and claimed that he lost all the tools of his trade on the ship. He had already been gifted £12.10.0 by his company to replace his lost clothing but wanted to claim £10 compensation for his tools so he could get a plumbing job in Australia. Such a simple request was not so simple; there followed weeks of inter-departmental memoranda trying to work out who was responsible for assessing and paying the claims. Snowden's claim ended up on acting Prime Minister Arthur Fadden's desk, who decided that the Mercantile Marine office was to process any applications. Financial help was also available from the King George's Fund for Sailors who voted £500 to help relieve hardship arising from the loss of possessions.

The twenty Polish survivors from *Batory* were to become a problem to the authorities. They had been dismissed by *Batory*'s captain for various reasons of laziness, disobedience or misdemeanours. Initially, nobody was willing to take responsibility for them after they arrived in Sydney; the Polish Consul General said he was not in a position to help financially and the Orient Steam Navigation Company, the local agents for *Batory*'s owners, disclaimed any liability for their costs because they had been passengers on *Rangitane*. The Department of Labour and Industry were made guardians of the Poles in the hope that the costs could ultimately be recovered from their shipping company or government. It was agreed that the Poles would be treated in the same way as British evacuees from a Baltic state, namely that they would be eligible for a grant of up to £2.10.0 per week to cover maintenance while they had no means to finance themselves. As soon as they left Australia, received their own funds or found employment, the payments would stop.

The Polish survivors consisted of seven men and thirteen women, all of whom wanted to stay in Australia. But they were to cause many difficulties: they collectively claimed that they should continue receiving wages or compensation from *Batory*'s owners and not have to work, while the men complained that they had been sent to a seaman's institute while other survivors had been accommodated in hotels and boarding houses. There was also concern about the health of the women, most of whom had some form of medical treatment, and their unwillingness to find jobs involving domestic service. After much debate it was agreed that the Polish women would be granted a three month right to stay in Australia. Four of the seven men were also allowed a temporary right to stay, one had disappeared and the remaining two were interned but later released on parole.

Discussions about the fate of the Poles continued throughout 1941. The Polish government in exile in London were most insistent that all seven men should be returned to Britain to join the armed forces. The Polish Consul-General in Sydney recanted, saying that only five should be sent back immediately. One of the others had been diagnosed with a heart condition and the other was to marry one of the Polish stewardesses. Another insisted that he had already fought in the air force in Britain, a claim which was roundly denied by his own government. The five were eventually repatriated to an unknown fate.

A number of the survivors spent many weeks in St. Vincent's hospital in Sydney. Florence Mundie who had lost an arm and had born serious facial injury was to take many months to recover. But some were unexpected patients. Geoffrey Barley was rushed to hospital with a burst appendix; having lost over forty pounds in weight, he was to remain in hospital for three months.

Betsy Sandbach and Geraldine Edge were amazed at the kindness and hospitality they experienced in Sydney. They received donations from the Red Cross, had free meals at the Royal Over-Seas League club and were invited to tea with Lord and Lady Gowrie. In return, they took part in fund raising events in which they gave short talks to various organisations. Captain Upton and CORB escort Margaret Osborne did their share of morale boosting: they were invited by the Australian Broadcasting Commission (ABC) to make speeches at a parade to raise money for radio sets for the Australian infantry camps. Upton was specifically asked 'if you could end with a word of warning to the audience in regard to gossiping about ships' movements' and his script had to be submitted and approved. Margaret Osborne made four similar broadcasts but her arch-enemy, Starr Stuart, wanted to get in on the act, and tried to persuade ABC to let her say something on the radio. In her letter to her Mother, Osborne wrote:

> Those two swine the Stuarts are pretty well taped by Sydney society. I think we have none of us spared them when talking to anyone at all influential and directly Mr. Fairfax heard what I had to tell him about their disgusting behaviour he immediately cooked their goose at a press conference. Yesterday the ABC told us that her scriptwriting for broadcasting was slanderous in parts and crazy in others so she has not been allowed to go on the air at all. Apparently she was furious and her wrath was made even greater when she heard that I had already made two broadcasts, was to do a third, and am now to do a fourth.

Captain Upton had many other jobs to complete. He wrote to every organisation involved in the repatriation of the survivors. A particularly poignant letter was sent to *Nellore*'s Captain Fred Colvin, in which praise was heaped on him and his crew. Little did they know that *Nellore* would be torpedoed and sunk in 1944 by a Japanese submarine. Captain Colvin and ninety-six crew and passengers were to perish.

On Monday 5 January a service was held in St. Andrew's Cathedral, Sydney for those who had died as a result of the actions of the raiders. Newspapers reported that the cathedral was packed with at least 500 people, ranging from the Premier, the Governor-General and government ministers, to hundreds of survivors, many of whom were still unshaven and wearing the same clothes as when they were rescued. Many had bandages and splints and had to be helped to their pews. The service was led by Archbishop Mowll and a particularly moving address made by Dr. R. G. Macintyre, chairman of the Overseas Children Citizens' Committee, referring to the deaths of the CORB escorts.

On a lighter note, a special Rangitane Ball was held on 17 January at the Trocadero dance hall, hosted by Sir Thomas and Lady Gordon in support of the King George's Fund for Sailors. The occasion witnessed a mix of officers in smart dress uniforms and a few survivors who had been persuaded to maintain their wild beards and hairstyles. The ball raised an additional £200 for the sailors' fund.

The survivors finally dispersed, some returned to England but many stayed in Australia and New Zealand. The men were in a difficult situation: they had all signed the parole agreement and they did not know how they stood legally with the military authorities.

Chapter 12

The Parole Problem

The legality or otherwise of the parole signed by the raiders' prisoners was to tax many minds in the first few months of 1941. The wording of the pledge was:

> We the undersigned do hereby give our word of honour and declare solemnly that on our release we will bear neither arms nor undertake military actions against Germany and her allies during the present hostilities. By breach of this promise we realise we are liable to capital punishment.

The form of wording in the pledge was clearly an attempt to take advantage of the provisions of Convention XI of the 1907 Hague Convention which stated:

> REGULATIONS REGARDING THE CREWS OF ENEMY MERCHANT SHIPS CAPTURED BY A BELLIGERENT
> Article 5. When an enemy merchant ship is captured by a belligerent, such of its crew as are nationals of a neutral State are not made prisoners of war. The same rule applies in the case of the captain and officers likewise nationals of a neutral State, if they promise formally in writing not to serve on an enemy ship while the war lasts.
>
> Article 6. The captain, officers, and members of the crew, when nationals of the enemy State, are not made prisoners of war, on condition that they make a formal promise in writing, not to undertake, while hostilities last, any service connected with the operations of the war.
>
> Article 7. The names of the persons retaining their liberty under the conditions laid down in Article 5, paragraph 2, and in Article 6, are notified by the belligerent captor to the other

> belligerent. The latter is forbidden knowingly to employ the said persons.
>
> Article 8. The provisions of the three preceding articles do not apply to ships taking part in the hostilities.

Article 6 was to be the most relevant to the prisoners. It is interesting that early in 1940 standing orders had already addressed the question of armed forces personnel signing a similar pledge. For example, War Office order 132/40 said:

> The attention of all officers is directed to the fact that in accordance with the custom of the Service no officer who is taken prisoner of war is justified in giving his parole. An officer will, therefore, refuse his parole and will accept internment as a prisoner of war until he affects his escape, or is released or exchanged.

But there was no equivalent order affecting the merchant seamen who were considered to be civilians, not members of the fighting forces. The first questions on the subject of the status of merchant seamen were raised by the French government in March 1940 in a letter to the Foreign Office in London. It asked for the British government's view firstly on 'whether a belligerent has the right to detain merchant seamen who have fallen into its power' and '...whether merchant seamen, if detained, should be treated as prisoners of war or as civilian internees.' It was clear from the context of the letter that the French government wanted to detain German merchant seamen as prisoners of war.

The reply dated 11 May, 1940 from the Foreign Office was blunt. It gave two reasons why they felt that Article 6 was not binding in the present war: the Germans had not offered the crew of a trawler, the *Caldew*, the option of signing an undertaking, therefore breaching and nullifying that part of the Hague Convention, and that the Germans had no right to expect for their seamen special privileges while their submarines continue to attack British merchant vessels, endangering the lives of British seamen. It then said that although German seamen were in a broad sense prisoners of war, it was impractical to treat them as such under the Hague Convention and that they would be interned in civilian camps. However, the UK's true intent in 1940 came to light in a letter dated 15 February 1941, stating Foreign Secretary Anthony Eden's views of the time to the Admiralty: 'the position is that, so long as the Germans are content to release prisoners while His Majesty's Government do not, His Majesty's Government are getting the best of both worlds.'

This confirmed that German merchant seamen were not to be offered an Article 6 undertaking and was followed up in an instruction to that effect on 27 May 1940, to all services, supplemented by a later circular confirming that it also applied to Italian merchant seamen. The matter rested there until the UK, Australian and New Zealand authorities were inundated by questions from many dozens of Emirau survivors who, having pledged their parole, wanted to know where they stood legally.

The first response by New Zealand was to suggest that the problem was a moral, not a legal one. In their cable to Australia and the Dominion Office in London they said that they were inclined to the view that 'these people have rightly or wrongly pledged their word in order to obtain release, their pledge should be honoured and they should not be required or indeed allowed to undertake military or naval service.' The cable added 'The question of defensively armed merchant vessels is of greater difficulty' and asked the opinions of the other governments.

The question of service on Defensively Equipped Merchant ships (DEMS) was, indeed, problematic. As has already been noted, *Rangitane* was a merchant ship manned by merchant seamen but was armed with a stern gun operated by DEMS trained personnel. George Wilson was a Royal Naval Voluntary Reservist and Donald Windrush was a Royal Naval gunner, assisted by Merchant Seaman/Gunners Clarence Henderson and

A. Mills. It was a requirement that all DEMS military personnel should sign-on as employees of the shipping line to ensure that they came under the direct orders of the ship's master. It also added a degree of legitimacy to claims that any captured DEMS crew should be treated as civilians. The underlying question was whether any ship armed with a gun for defensive purposes was classed as a war ship. If so, then any survivors who later served in any capacity on a DEMS ship were technically in breach of their pledge. In the early part of the war, this was not a major issue because relatively few merchant ships were armed and survivors could elect to re-join the merchant navy on an unarmed ship. By the end of the war over sixty percent would be armed. It did not matter how the Allies perceived the status of DEMS ships: in the end it was down to the individual commander of an enemy warship who determined how prisoners would be classified and treated.

The Australian Naval Office initially agreed that it was a moral, not legal, problem and that signatories to the pledge should not be compelled to join the fighting services. They disagreed about preventing them from serving, saying that they should be allowed to join voluntarily, including service on DEMS ships. The Naval Office rather naively suggested that DEMS ships 'were in a different category to warships' as if this subtlety would influence the enemy. But Australia made an important observation, saying that they were concerned that merchant seamen were being allowed to give their parole to the enemy, while the armed services strictly forbade it under standing orders. They suggested that in future nobody should be allowed to give any form of undertaking for their freedom.

The matter did not rest there and views changed. After consulting his New Zealand counterpart, Australia's Prime Minister Fadden cabled the Foreign Office in London with further views, saying that the problem was neither moral nor legal, but political. While still agreeing that the British need no longer be bound by Article 6, he said that the moral argument of the parole did not apply because the prisoners were given no genuine choice: they would have been put ashore anyway. In addition, he said that the threat of capital punishment was unreal because 'It is true that although international law admits a right to inflict capital punishment for breach of parole in certain aggravated cases, but the implied penalty here is so disproportionate to the offence envisaged as to deprive it not merely of legal but also of moral sanction.'

Fadden continued to outline his reasoning that the problem was only a political one. He said

> The fact is, as we see it, that the extraction of the undertaking was merely a form of intimidation. It is unlikely that the German Commander concerned seriously believed that the promise would be observed for reasons of honour: what he did was to convey a threat in a way best calculated to impress each individual. In our view, it is this aspect which should determine Governmental attitude. To leave the matter to individual conscience, still more to enforce observance of undertaking, as New Zealand Government are inclined to suggest, would, in our opinion, amount to acquiescence in a particularly arrogant act of intimidation. On grounds of general policy, we consider that the creation of so dangerous a precedent, having regard to German methods of warfare, should not be entertained.

His conclusion was that, in principle, nothing should be done which could be construed as declaring the parole to be valid but in the same breath he said 'In practice, reasonable care could no doubt be taken not to expose individuals affected, for their own protection, to undue risk of recapture.' Unfortunately the Navy Minister still recorded his dissent saying:

> No doubt a case can be made out that the undertaking was given in duress – but it still remains true that it was given; the contention that there was no alternative is weak; there was an alternative – Just what would have happened we cannot say –

> the refusal might have meant detention on raider – or something more drastic. In any case those who gave the undertaking thought it wise – expedient – to do so. They did it with their eyes open: now it is said that they did it under duress and so their undertaking is not binding. I disagree.

Anthony Eden then suggested that pledges given within the wording and spirit of Article 6 should be honoured but any undertaking made outside the bounds of Article 6, including a promise not to serve on defensively equipped merchant ships, should not be honoured.

Clearly, the various opinions and disagreements were getting nowhere and the months of wrangling can now been seen as diplomatic dithering. The solution was a simple compromise: the allied governments would unofficially renounce Article 6 and would intern enemy merchant seamen. If the enemy nations released British merchant seamen, so much the better, and Eden would get his best of both worlds. Unofficially, the governments would be quite happy for the *Rangitane* and other ships' survivors to be allowed to stay well away from potentially dangerous situations and leave it to their own consciences whether to engage in wartime support roles, including service on DEMS ships.

As a result of the indecisions, the Admiralty decided to re-issue its standing orders to clarify the position for the Royal Navy. Order 106/41 stated:

> 1. Officers and men taken prisoner by the enemy are not to give their parole not to attempt to escape. Nor are they voluntarily to give an undertaking that if they are released they will take no further part in hostilities.
> 2. The Admiralty will countenance the giving of parole or of such an undertaking by an officer or man only if he is required by the enemy to give it in circumstances which do not admit to refusal.

3. In general, officers who are interned in neutral countries are also to regard themselves as forbidden to give parole. Their Lordships, however, will be prepared to consider departures from this rule in particular cases, and any naval officer interned in a neutral country who wishes to receive permission to give parole should make application accordingly through H.M. Representative in the country concerned.

A good example of how the parole policy was implemented for merchant seamen was the case of William Menzies. He had gained a DEMS certificate in early 1940 and had been *Baltannic*'s First Officer returning home on *Rangitane* when she was sunk. On his return to England he wanted to re-qualify on the DEMS training ship HMS *Flying Fox* berthed in Bristol. He had signed the parole undertaking and he asked Reginald Lawrence, commander of *Flying Fox,* what his position was. Lawrence advised him that he was obliged to honour his pledge but referred his decision to the Admiralty for confirmation. For once, the Admiralty responded quickly and to the point: anybody who had made the pledge was only to be given a shore based support role. Bobby Clint, a young steward on *Rangitane* arrived back in Liverpool and was summoned to the army recruiting station. When he explained his predicament, he was told he could either have a non-combatant army role and stay in England, or he could re-join the merchant marine. Bobby went back to sea. Henry Williams, *Rangitane*'s second mate preferred not to return to England, stayed in Wellington and was given a shore-based stevedore's job.

Tug Wilson, another *Baltannic* crewman, made the decision for himself. Originally from a Yorkshire farming family, he decided to go to New Zealand after his rescue from Emirau. He wanted to stay in the merchant marine and signed up on an unarmed cargo ship, content that he was abiding by his pledge. Unfortunately, it was decided that the ship should be armed and manned by DEMS gunners. Wilson made up his mind quickly:

he gave in his notice and found an onshore engineering job, later training as a pilot and being known as the Flying Farmer.

Fred Kingsford made a different decision: originally from Middlesex, he stayed on in Australia and joined the army, serving in the 148th Motor Transport Column delivering supplies to the troops in New Guinea. He said 'I figured that the Germans wouldn't be looking for a merchant sailor in the Aussie army.' He later served on HMAS *Napier* escorting an American aircraft carrier in the Pacific. For the rest of his life Fred Kingsford kept the bamboo spoon he made for himself while captive on *Kulmerland.*

Captain Upton was subject to the same rules as the other merchant seamen. His captaincy of *Rangitane* was to have been his last trip in the merchant marine; being a Royal Naval Reservist, he had been called-up to join the navy on his return to England. When he eventually returned home he commuted daily from Hove to HMS *President,* permanently berthed on the Thames.

Other survivors had decisions made for them. *Rangitane*'s RNZAF recruits, who returned home in January, 1941 were informed that they were booked on another ship departing for England on 1 February to continue their training. When the issue of their parole was raised there was again political dithering, until they were finally told to stay in New Zealand. Ian MacLean and Tom Newland ended up training new air recruits while some others decided to go into farming, a reserved occupation.

Frank Ellison was one of the prisoners transported to POW camp in Germany. He always said that he thought that he might have been lucky; had he not been a POW, he might have been a casualty later in the war. But Frank knew nothing of the parole. Had he signed it, and had he been released on Emirau, the parole would have protected him for the remainder of the war.

Chapter 13

The 1941 Inquiry

The New Zealand Government was quick to respond to the public outcry over the allegations being made by the survivors. Terms of reference were issued as early as 30 January, 1941 to enquire into and report on:

(a) The circumstances surrounding the loss of the steamship *Holmwood*, the motor-vessel *Rangitane,* the motor-vessel *Vinni*, and the steamship *Komata* ;
(b) The question whether there have been any leakages, either directly or indirectly, from New Zealand of information relating to the movements of ships; and, if so, the facts, relating to such leakages.

The Commission of Inquiry started less than a week later in Wellington, headed by John Callan, a well known Justice in the Supreme Court. He was assisted by William Perry, President of the Law Society, Captain F. A. Macindoe, Captain E. Rotherham and Mr. T. F. Anderson. The Solicitor-General, H. H. Cornish was the master of ceremonies, summoning, organising, ushering and cross-examining a total of ninety-three witnesses including thirty-four survivors from the various ships concerned.

Cornish was eloquent and almost Churchillian in his opening statement:

> No commission has ever been set up in this country having a more important task. So far as the subject matter is concerned, this commission is unique. It is certainly unique in this country and I do not know of any similar commission that has been set up during this war in any other member of the British Commonwealth. It may be that the findings of this commission will be of the greatest benefit, not only to this Dominion, but to other parts of the Commonwealth - perhaps to the English-

> speaking world – and the fruits of this inquiry may be seen, one, two or three years after the present time, because on the safety of shipping, I think it is conceded, depends the success of our war effort.

His first task was to raise the question of whether the inquiry should be held *in camera,* not only excluding the public and press, but preventing witnesses or anybody else speaking on the matter outside the inquiry. He argued that the subject matter involving secret wartime procedures could not be discussed in public but it would also give the witnesses confidence to say things they may otherwise not want to say in open proceedings. There was an objection to this view: F. P. Walsh, a firebrand trade unionist representing both seamen and industrial workers, made a strong plea that the proceedings should in public, to demonstrate that the issues were being treated openly and fairly. He was concerned that his members, particularly the seamen, should not be used as scapegoats. He also said that he, personally, should sit with the Commission and have the power to call and cross-examine witnesses. His request was refused on both counts: the inquiry was held *in camera.* The fact that Walsh had called the fairness of the inquiry into question was to influence proceedings: Justice Callan later said 'In view of our firm attitude of sitting *in camera* and not allowing Mr. Walsh, we have to watch our step closely.' It is somewhat ironic that, when Walsh was later called as a witness, he wanted an assurance that anything he said would not be released to the public. He said 'I do not want it said outside that I gave this evidence.'

Many letters started arriving at the Commission from people who had information or theories about how the Germans received their information about shipping movements. Some were sensible but many were fanciful. Some were obviously from people with old scores to settle. Cornish suggested that, as Solicitor-General, his staff could screen out the good from the bad. Justice Callan disliked that: he said that some letters were already laying blame with government departments and it would be wrong for another department to do the screening.

The very first line of enquiry was on a burning issue that had been alluded to in the press: why, when *Holmwood*'s Captain Miller first identified the first suspicious ship, did he not follow the standard procedure to transmit a warning? That action may have persuaded Captain Upton to return *Rangitane* to Auckland. The standard raider warning was QQQQ followed by the name of the ship sending the warning and her longitude and latitude position and, if possible the nature of the suspicion

The procedural aspect of Miller's evidence would be the most difficult of the whole inquiry. While witnesses normally gave evidence individually and without representation, Miller knew that he was to be criticised and had been warned that his evidence would be carefully cross-examined. Because his personal and professional reputations were at stake, Miller had been told by Cornish that he could be accompanied by legal counsel.

Commodore Parry, Chief of the Naval Staff, was the first to give evidence, outlining how *Holmwood* was captured and how it resulted in *Rangitane* not being recalled to port. Captain James Miller and his counsel Mr. Kirkcaldie then entered to give evidence.

Miller said that it was about 7.25 a.m. when Second Officer Claude Clarke woke him to report that a ship was approaching fast astern on the port quarter about two miles away. Miller left his cabin next to the wheelhouse in his pyjamas to see the ship had Japanese colours on her sides and was flying three hoists of international signal flags obscured by its funnel. He returned to his cabin to put clothes over his pyjamas, and retrieved his international signal book to read the flag signals. While trying to read the flags, the ship, now on his port beam, dropped its sides to expose her guns and Swastikas were draped over the Japanese colours and another was run up the yardarm.

Miller said that he told his helmsman, Donald McLeod, to turn two points to starboard to move away from the raider and instructed Angus Campbell, his chief officer, to throw the secret naval papers overboard. When Miller was asked why he did not transmit the raider warning message as required by naval orders, he gave the following reasons:

1. He was the only wireless operator on board and that his duty was to remain on the bridge in command of his vessel;
2. A wireless message would be wasted because his transmitter would not reach the mainland and that the Chatham Island wireless station, only forty-eight miles away, was not manned until 9 a.m. He also assumed that there would be no ships in the area to pick up and relay a message.
3. He had had no wireless practice since the start of the war because use was banned while at sea. He said that it would take too long to switch on, warm up, and transmit the message.
4. The raider was so close that it was at point blank range and would have destroyed *Holmwood* with its first shot and he feared for the lives of the women and children passengers.

Some of these reasons appeared plausible, given the very short notice Miller claimed he had been given and the close proximity of the raider. But Clarke was to disagree. He said that he had first seen the ship coming over the horizon after 7 a.m. and did not become suspicious until about 7.10 a.m. when he roused Miller in his cabin. Miller said that Clarke was wrong and had waited at least twenty-five minutes before calling him, which would have given ample time to transmit a warning.

Donald McLeod had been on the helm until 6 a.m. when he was relieved by Clarke and told to erect some ventilation chutes for the sheep. McLeod said he returned to the bridge at 7.10 a.m.

when Clarke, for some reason, went aft for five to ten minutes, then returned to tell McLeod that he had seen the suspicious ship about five miles away. McLeod said he was surprised: over four years of sailing between the Chathams and mainland, he had only ever seen two other ships. They discussed who it could be, possibly SS *Hector*, one of the navy's auxiliary cruisers. McLeod claimed that it was at this stage that Miller was summoned from his cabin.

Clarke's version was that he had left the bridge before 7 a.m. to go and feed the horse which was in a box in the aft hatch. He said that he fed the horse and was fixing a boat cover when he first saw the suspicious ship about five miles away on the aft quarter. He claimed that he returned to the bridge by 7.10 a.m. and called Captain Miller with whom he had a discussion. He then said to McLeod that he was going to the stern to hoist the ensign.

Two other witnesses, Angus Campbell and Fred Abernethy gave contrasting timings of having spoken to Miller and Clarke during this period. At the inquiry, Justice Callan was irritated by the conflicting statements and inconsistent timings. In the end, the inquiry's report rejected everybody's timings, saying that that the ship must have been visible by 7 a.m. and even by 7.30 a.m. it would still have been two miles away. The view was that Miller would have had at least forty-five minutes in which to raise the alarm, had he been roused as soon as the vessel was seen.

In reviewing the evidence, there were two possible scenarios for what happened: Clarke may have seen the first signs of the ship coming over the horizon around 7 a.m., and, while waiting to see what developed, went aft to feed the horse. By the time he finished, the ship was much closer and it was then that he called Miller at 7.25 a.m. The more likely explanation is that Clarke went to feed the horse, then seeing the ship on the horizon, returned to the bridge and called Miller sometime after 7.10 a.m. Miller then took too long dressing and trying to read the flag signals. In both cases, Miller considered the raider to be too close to risk raising the alarm.

The inquiry naturally did not have access to the raiders' log books in 1941. However, *Komet*'s commander Robert Eyssen published his wartime memoirs in 1960, including a detailed account, with times, of *Holmwood*'s capture. At first sight, the times appear to be inconsistent with those presented at the inquiry. For example, while most witnesses at the inquiry said that *Holmwood* actually stopped her engines by 8 a.m., Eyssen said that it was 7.09 a.m., about fifty minutes earlier. But it is interesting that, while the inquiry concluded that the raider must have been visible at about 7 a.m., Eyssen recorded his first sighting of *Holmwood* at 6.10 a.m., about fifty minutes earlier again. This suggests that the absolute times are different but the relative times of individual incidents are similar. Eyssen recorded that he first raised his signal flags and exposed his guns at 6.40 a.m., thirty-one minutes after first seeing *Holmwood.* Using the inquiry's times, this would be 7.31 a.m., a time which accords with the inquiry's deductions. It is surprising that Eyssen said that when he raised his colours he was 4000 metres away, equivalent to just over two nautical miles, agreeing with the inquiry's estimate. Why the clocks on *Holmwood* and *Komet* should disagree by fifty minutes is not known. Allowances of plus or minus five minute differences could be made on each ship suggesting an aggregate error of plus or minus ten minutes, but a fifty minute difference appears excessive. While it is probable that *Komet*'s recorded times were reasonably accurate through naval discipline, it begs the question of how many of *Holmwood*'s times were observed and the accuracy of her clock. It is interesting to see that when *Rangitane* was first challenged, Eyssen recorded *Komet*'s time as 3.00 a.m. but Upton recorded it on *Rangitane* as 3.40 a.m., a difference of forty, not fifty minutes.

The inquiry report was extremely critical of Miller and Clark. Miller was reprimanded for not getting a message away despite the circumstances and Clarke for not keeping a proper watch while his captain was off-duty and not calling the captain earlier. Justice Callan gave stern warnings to a number of witnesses about lax security procedures on board and in the report said 'while relaxed practices may have been normal in peacetime, wartime conditions demanded greater vigilance.'

Miller was treated harshly: he had taken the brunt of the blame in the press and he was then criticised by the inquiry. It is clear that he was faced with an impossible situation: the first he knew of the raider was only a few minutes before he was staring down the barrel of a naval gun. If he had started to raise the alarm, there would have been an immediate reprisal at point blank range and he had concern for the women and children on board. The report acknowledged that his situation was impossible but said, in effect, that war was war, and broadcasting a warning took priority, no matter what the consequences were. It said that the dilemma existed because the women and children had been placed in a compromising situation by being allowed to travel in potentially dangerous circumstances. It demanded that such travel should only be sanctioned under extreme circumstances.

Captain Miller was represented throughout his cross-examination by his legal counsel Mr Kirkcaldie. No other witness at the inquiry was so represented. Towards the end of the inquiry when it became clear that Miller was to bear the brunt of the criticism, Kirkcaldie made a valiant effort, clearly with the benefit of hindsight, to demonstrate that the Admiralty instructions relating to suspicious vessels had, in fact, been followed by Miller.

One Admiralty instruction, delivered to *Holmwood* on 22 November, 1940, only a week before she was sunk, said

> To ensure the rounding up of enemy raiders it is essential they are reported by wireless telegraph whatever the cost. The enemy is aware of this provision and his first object is to get close enough to shoot away your wireless aerial. It is of the utmost importance

> that a wireless telegraph report is made out before he can get in a position to do this.

Kirkcaldie argued that the precise wording of the last sentence had been obeyed by Miller because the raider was already in a position to shoot away the wireless before Miller was in a position to act. This subtle legal interpretation was technically correct and the inquiry's report resulted in future wording of the instruction being modified.

Kirkcaldie also raised another legal argument: he said that the Shipping Control Emergency Regulations 1939 made a number of all-encompassing demands on those in charge of vessels. These included the adherence, for example, to Admiralty instructions, as and when they were issued, on whatever subject. Such instructions had to be complied with 'at all reasonable speed, perils of the sea, and restraint of princes alone excepted.' This was, and still is, a legal term in maritime contracts to absolve the master of a vessel of his duty if he was unable to comply with an instruction because, for example, of interference by a government. Typically, this would be because of quarantine, embargo, confiscation of a ship or seizure under a state of war. Kirkcaldie argued that Miller was within the law because he was under the forced orders of an enemy state. As it was, Miller was not facing prosecution, it was only his professional and personal reputation at stake so the legal argument was more hypothetical than crucial.

The inquiry made a number of recommendations arising out of the circumstance of the capture of *Holmwood* and new regulations and instructions were issued to ship operators in the following months. Unfortunately for Miller, his inquisition did not end there; he was to be interrogated about his firm belief that the Germans had acquired secret information and knew exactly where to find *Rangitane.*

Chapter 14

Leakage of information

The most damaging allegation was made by *Holmwood*'s crew and passengers. They claimed that their captors had told them that they would be capturing a large two-funnelled ship on the following day. This prediction, if truly made, evidently came to fruition. Further claims, particularly by Captain Eyssen, that he knew in advance the routes taken by *Rangitane* on her outward and return journeys, led Captain Upton to believe firmly that security had been compromised. While the intelligence services would still have investigated the allegations carefully, the fact that survivors Judge Stuart and his wife made such forceful public statements meant that their particular allegations were investigated thoroughly. The inquiry report said 'In view of the offices Mr. Stuart has held, and to which he has been appointed, we have considered with particular care the record of what he has said and the conclusions to which he came.'

The inquiry heard from a number of witnesses about how sea passages were planned and executed under wartime conditions. Ships would normally sail the shortest route in peacetime, usually a great circle route, but wartime Admiralty regulations required all British registered ships to follow routes prescribed by the Naval Control Service Officer (NCSO) at the point of departure. There were a number of reasons for this: it would stop ships always taking the same route, which would become known to an enemy; it ensured that ships used approach channels that had been swept for mines, and it would provide the authorities with some knowledge of the location of a ship in the event of a mishap.

The procedure was that a company wanting to route a vessel out of local territorial waters would first inform the local NCSO of the date and time of departure and intended destination. The captain would visit the NCSO's office a few days before departure to be given the route to be taken. This would take the form of a chart and a printed set of co-ordinates for waypoints through which the ship must pass. The captain would be able to discuss the route with the NCSO and, when agreed, the list would be sealed in an envelope, marked as secret, locked in the ship's safe and only opened after sailing. On completion of his journey the captain would hand over the route to the NCSO at his destination.

The NCSO at the departure port would send the route via teleprinter to the Staff Officer Intelligence (SOI) in Wellington, where it would be passed to the marine shipping room coordinating all ship movements around New Zealand. The NCSO also sent it to his counterpart in the destination port and a Vesca telegram addressed to Fairmiss in the Admiralty in the U.K. Vesca was a merchant ship reporting system used in the First World War and revived in 1939 which enabled a global picture of ship movements to be maintained.

There was much discussion at the inquiry about how the route instructions might fall into enemy hands. Commander Bingley, the naval officer in charge of Auckland, said that he had personally issued the routing instruction to Upton for his final voyage. He said that since the start of the war, there had been only four standard routes printed in four separate secret books for the Auckland to Panama leg of the homeward journey. These were numbered BA1, BA2, BA3 and BA4 and were all at least 100 miles from the normal direct route. Each had the latitude and longitude of seven waypoints printed on fifty tear-off slips in the book, printed in the U.K. before the war. Until August 1940 Bingley decided which route a ship was to take, select the appropriate book, tear out the pre-printed slip of co-ordinates and give it to the captain before he sailed.

Bingley said that in August 1940 he became concerned that there was insufficient variation in the standard routes. He started instructing captains to follow prescribed offsets to the north or south. He said that he instructed a ship to follow one hundred miles north of BA1 on the day prior to *Rangitane*'s departure and the *Waiotira* to sail sixty miles south of BA2 on the following day. The offset routes were given to the captains as recalculated co-ordinates typewritten on a slip of paper. Bingley said that sometimes he would revert to one of the four standard routes and that one of these had been given to Upton for his departure.

At the inquiry, Upton said that he was uneasy about using a standard pre-printed route which had been in existence for eighteen months. This was confirmed by Bingley who said that he explained to Upton that the route had not been used for a long time, but that Upton was at liberty to devise his own route which he could submit for approval. Upton later contacted Bingley to say that he believed BA1 to be the safest after all, but that some of the waypoints, particularly the first, should be omitted.

Upton received his final instructions and, according to Bingley, was told verbally to sail a Mercator route, not a great circle route. These were the two methods used for ocean navigation. A great circle route is the shortest distance between any two points on the globe but requires continuous readjustment of a ship's compass bearing. A Mercator route, also known as a Rhumb Line, is a longer route but has a constant compass bearing which could be measured directly from a sea chart drawn using the Mercator projection.

Despite Bingley's instruction to follow a Mercator route, Upton said in his evidence that he decided to take a great circle route, claiming that standing orders allowed him to choose one or the other. But Upton's statement is puzzling because, had he followed the great circle route to his first waypoint, *Rangitane* would have been at least fifty miles off course to the north after sailing for less than two days. This would not have been within normal navigational tolerances: it was standard practice for regular positional fixes to be taken and course adjustments made to allow for wind and current drift. Fixes made by sextant would normally be expected to be within one minute of arc (one nautical mile) accuracy. Other calculations show that if Upton had sailed a great circle course to miss out his first waypoint or even all waypoints, *Rangitane* was still a long way off course when she was sunk.

One possible explanation might have been that for very long trans-ocean journeys it was common practice for a great circle route to be divided into a series of much shorter legs, which could be navigated using constant Mercator bearings for each leg. The navigation officer would calculate the latitude on the great circle for each ten degree increment in longitude, and then sail a constant Mercator bearing to that latitude. The bearing would then be changed for the next ten degree increment of longitude, and so on. It can be shown that if Upton was heading for the 170 degree meridian on the great circle to his first waypoint, he would still have been a long way off course.

The most likely explanation is that, after all, Upton actually sailed the Mercator route to his first waypoint as specified by Bingley, despite having told the inquiry differently. If this was the case, it can be shown that *Rangitane* was less than eight miles south out of position where she was caught, a much more likely error for a professional navigator, and representing approximately one degree on the ship's heading. Upton's evidence, which was given over many days of intense questioning, was often varied and confused. For example, he said that insurance companies may not pay out if a captain had not followed an NCSO's specified course, yet he claimed that he had ignored Bingley's instructions and sailed a great circle course.

The riddle is whether the Germans knew in advance of *Rangitane*'s intended course and, therefore, how to find her. The suggestion that they knew was made by Captain Eyssen on the day that *Holmwood* was captured on 25 November. During the afternoon, Captain Miller was interrogated by the Germans about his knowledge of naval codes. Miller was surprised that they knew that, prior to setting sail at 2.30 a.m., he had drafted and handed in two signals to the Chatham Islands wireless office for transmission when the operator started his shift at 9 a.m. One message was in merchant navy code to his ship's owner and the other in plain text to Lyttelton, informing them of his cargo. *Komet*'s wireless monitoring had obviously picked up the transmissions after the Chatham office had opened, and therefore after *Holmwood* had been captured. Eyssen claimed full knowledge of the content of the plain text message but asked Miller for the plain text of the coded message. Miller played the innocent, saying that it was his agent who had drafted and sent the message. It can be deduced from this that the raiders did not have, or had not yet used, any code books to decode the message.

Miller was also asked by Eyssen the name of the cruiser which, he claimed, was moored at Lyttelton, asking specifically if it was HMAS *Sydney*. Miller said that he had no idea, and Eyssen replied that it did not matter because he had some friends aboard her who would find out her name. With the benefit of hindsight, this was a naive and hardly credible statement by Eyssen, but it had a profound effect on Miller. Eyssen was clearly playing with Miller, feeding him snippets of information, gleaned mainly from the captured Chatham Island's postbag and wireless records, but giving the impression that it was supplied by supposed agents in New Zealand. It was inevitable that everything which happened thereafter would fuel Miller's suspicions. Miller suspected that there was a fourth raider involved in *Holmwood*'s capture and which was operating close to the mainland shore. He said that a plane from that raider had obviously spotted the cruiser at Lyttelton and had relayed the information to Eyssen on *Komet*. Other witnesses at the inquiry made the same claim but none could provide the source of the evidence, other than from that which Miller believed.

Miller also testified that on the day following their capture, the German seamen started clearing stores from a hold adjacent to captives' quarters. When Miller jokingly asked whether it was to let them have a dance, one German replied that they were making room 'for plenty of friends tomorrow.' The remark meant little to Miller at the time but, following *Rangitane*'s capture the next day, it became another significant reason for Miller to suspect subterfuge. Unfortunately no other witness could independently substantiate what had been said.

Captains Miller and Upton were to offer significant conflicting evidence to the inquiry. After *Rangitane* was captured, Upton was to share quarters with Miller and it was there that Upton claimed with certainty that he was told by Miller that the Germans knew they were going to capture 'a big two-funnelled steamer the next morning.' Miller strongly denied this, saying that he told Upton only that the hold had been cleared the previous day. It is unfortunate that it was Upton's version that was told and re-told by the prisoners over the following weeks: everybody was convinced that the raiders had been lying in wait. Indeed, Eyssen recited to Upton the exact times that *Rangitane* had cast-off at Auckland, had anchored off Rangitoto, and had finally set off on her journey. But Eyssen was mocking his captives: he told anybody who would listen that he knew the arrival and departure times of all ships around the Antipodes. He even spun a story that he had intercepted *Rangitane* two hours earlier than expected. Even this embellishment was rationalised by Upton and Miller as being the difference in time between *Rangitane* following a great circle course instead of a Mercator course. What they ignored was the fact that they would have been miles away from where they were found, had they taken a different course.

It is understandable that the only explanation the prisoners could find for what they thought was privileged information, was that the Germans were getting it illegally. The issues would have been discussed time and time again during the long hours that the prisoners were locked in the holds and suspicions would have converted into certainties. It is not surprising that when they were rescued and released, everybody had the same story to tell the press.

The inquiry devoted a substantial amount of time interrogating survivors, and gradually developed an understanding of how the suspicions fermented. Many of Eyssen's claims could be explained away as idle boasting based on snippets of information. The Chatham's postbag and records of wireless transmissions explained events related to *Holmwood*, while the timings of *Rangitane*'s departure were known to many of her crew and passengers. Mrs. Jefferey was one of the crew who was taken to the stricter prison regime on *Orion*. In evidence she said that over the first few days, every prisoner was formally interviewed by Captain Weyher and his officers. She said that she was appalled at how friendly some of the Polish men and women were with their captors, speaking to them in German while being interrogated and not reporting what had been said to the other prisoners. This seems to be plausible: it was known that at least two Polish men had been escorted by the police when they boarded *Rangitane* in Auckland and it is reasonable to deduce that they had more reason than others to divulge information.

The inquiry's report summed up Eyssen thus: 'The statements attributed to him seem to us to be more likely part of an attempt to impress his captives, and, through them to disseminate uneasiness and distrust in New Zealand, or they may have been manifestations of boastfulness and a taste for melodrama.' It continued: 'he took a good deal of trouble to impress them with his cleverness and omniscience.'

The inquiry carefully studied the statements of Judge Stuart and his wife. Unfortunately they did not appear in person for cross-examination: they had both returned to the U.K. before it was set up. Judge Stuart's statement said:

> They met the *Rangitane* by appointment. They knew exactly where to find her. They complained to Captain Upton that on the way to New Zealand, he had not followed the naval instructions, and they had therefore missed the ship; but they congratulated him on having followed the naval instructions on the way out as to the course. They had full information as to

> the amount of cargo and its nature before they took the ship, as to the course to be taken, and the delay of some hours taken by Captain Upton in the Hauraki Gulf. Find the men who know the cargo; find the men who know the naval course; find the men who could have seen the delay in the Hauraki Gulf. I suggest that those, if any, who figure on all three lists, whoever they are, should be interned for the duration of the war.

The inquiry dismissed Stuart's allegation, saying that he was evidently one of the persons whom the Germans had succeeded in deceiving. Stuart had words to say about the search aircraft which the Germans had seen later on the day that *Rangitane* had been sunk, but the aircraft had evidently not seen them:

> We were all ordered down below, and we thought it was the Yankee Clipper diverted. My sanity reeled at the fact. It is apparently undisputed that New Zealand planes saw us just as they saw the ships that sank the *Turakina*, and no further action was taken. I submit that the persons responsible for that lack of action should, in the interests of New Zealand, be placed under control for the duration of the war. I have the honour to state that I intend to make this recommendation to the Imperial Government, who will by then, I hope, have heard that New Zealand intends to act upon this basis.

The inquiry heard evidence from Oscar Garden, the pilot of the flying boat *Aotearoa,* which was the first aircraft on the scene. He described the weather conditions, visibility and difficulty in spotting a boat in open ocean. Other witnesses agreed that a ship is much more likely to see an aircraft, than an aircraft see a ship.

Captain Upton was asked to sum up his opinion of the Stuarts. He said:

> They are cracked. I think that they gave way under the mental strain for the time being. All the passengers who came in contact with him have not a good word for him and he has not a good word for any of the passengers. They were all "rabble"

> and "not fit to be associated with". My honest opinion of the Judge is that he was distinctly abnormal. A Judge of a High Court, landed on an island in pyjamas dirtier than any of the seamen or anyone else jumps off the end of the wharf and takes his pyjamas off in front of all hands, I would not say is normal.

Clarence Henderson, one of *Rangitane*'s gunners said that he played cards with Judge Stuart on the raider and became well acquainted with him. He said 'He was rather erratic sometimes. He always thought he knew best.' Henderson described how the Stuarts were fearful for their safety because they had been threatened by one of the *Holmwood* crew because '... this man evidently had communist tendencies.' Henderson said that Judge Stuart was going to have the man tried in Sydney for sedition and that when everybody was landed on the island, Stuart 'was going to dispense justice and he had letters which entitled him to dispense justice in any part of the Empire.'

The inquiry had obviously heard enough about Judge Stuart, saying in its report:

> The account generally given of Mr. Stuart by his fellow-captives conveys an unfavourable impression as to his accuracy and reliability. His recorded statement gives no reasons for his conclusions. We have been quite unable to discover any evidence in support of those conclusions. We therefore reject them.

Of course, the inquiry had no access to Weyher's and Eyssen's war diaries which were acquired by the Allies in 1945, nor to their individual memoirs published in 1955 and 1960 respectively. According to these, the German commanders were taken completely by surprise when they encountered *Rangitane* in the dark, in the middle of the ocean. Weyher referred to having difficulty deciding what sort of ship they had come across. He knew it was much bigger and probably much faster than his raider, but could not even establish which way it was travelling. He immediately assumed that it was a warship, that one of the other German ships must already have been seen by it, and that he would have no alternative but to engage it. Eyssen was of the same opinion and it was not until they started using searchlights that they found it was a large two-funnelled passenger liner.

It is acknowledged that some German memoirs published immediately after the war may have massaged the truth either for reasons of self-promotion, self-denial or fear of reprisal. But attitudes had changed by the mid-1950s and there is little reason to doubt the accuracy of the commanders' statements on encountering *Rangitane* by chance. As previously commented, Eyssen was a consummate boaster in his memoirs about his exploits but, equally, he was quite poignant in describing his disappointments and failures. Weyher was different; he was blunt and pragmatic and stated the facts as he saw them. Both commanders would have earned kudos if they had really acquired intelligence information to lie in wait and ambush *Rangitane*, but the reality is that it was all just the luck of the draw in war.

Chapter 15

The Aftermath

Strategic fallout

Releasing his prisoners was a good humanitarian act by Captain Eyssen, but a strategic blunder for Germany. The prisoners knew the exact *modus operandi* of the raiders. The professional seamen could estimate raider speeds, bearings and positions. They knew about the Japanese supplies and they could describe in detail the changes of disguise, armaments and firepower.

There is no doubt that the Japanese government must either have been complicit in, or conveniently overlooked, the fact that at least seven German supply ships had been replenished in Japanese ports in the latter half of 1940. One of these was *Kulmerland*, before she met with *Komet* and *Orion*. Japan must also have been aware that the supply ships were using Lamotrek in the Caroline Islands and Ailinglaplap Atoll in the Marshall Islands to meet and re-provision German raiders. Both of these were Japanese mandated territories and often referred to as 'land-based aircraft carriers.' Such use of a neutral port by a ship on active war duty was only allowed for a maximum of twenty-four hours, a period of time exceeded on a number of occasions.

While Japan had yet to enter the war, and was technically still neutral, the war clouds were darkening and the British security forces were becoming extremely uneasy about Japan's intentions. Germany and Japan could have kept their supply arrangements secret for much longer had *Komet*'s Captain Eyssen not insisted on releasing his prisoners on Emirau. If he had sent all his prisoners back to Germany, nobody would have been any the wiser about Japan's complicity. As it was, Allied relations with Japan deteriorated rapidly when the issue of supply, and Eyssen's attack on Nauru, were raised at diplomatic level. The Australian government enacted legislation requiring all foreign merchant vessels to give formal notice of their intention to enter coastal waters. There were months of diplomatic friction, resulting in Japan refusing to conform, despite the threat of seizure of her vessels. The Australian position was simple: the Germans had used Japanese disguises and they felt vindicated in arresting any unannounced ship showing Japanese colours. Relationships had effectively collapsed by mid-1941 and the number of Japanese traders to Australia and New Guinea area plummeted. Those Japanese ships that ventured into port found it virtually impossible to trade: where officialdom failed to deny port facilities, patriotic dock workers staged embargoes and refused to handle cargoes. German naval command (SKL) must have known of these problems and it is clear that any return to the region disguised as Japanese merchantmen would have invited immediate attention and retribution. By the end of 1941, there was no need for a German presence in the area; Japan consumed all of the defensive forces that Australia and New Zealand could muster.

Eyssen obviously knew that the raiders' operational information would quickly find its way into British hands. But one aspect of Eyssen's behaviour defies logic: his boasting and exaggeration. He told anyone who would listen that he had access to secret information about ship movements in the region and that his intelligence unit could decypher all British codes. His all-knowing attitude was clearly designed to unsettle his prisoners, but it must have been obvious that the security services would be alerted immediately after their release.

Disagreement over the release of the prisoners had clearly been the final straw in the relationship between Eyssen and Weyher. It is known that Weyher reported his disagreement to SKL and that Eyssen received an indirect rebuke when all raiders were quickly instructed never to release prisoners again. He was also castigated for the attacks at Nauru while flying Japanese colours. The damage had been done: the British merchant navy code was replaced on 3 January 1941, SKL intelligence units lost valuable time building new decrypts and the Allied security services started clamping down.

There were other strategically important after-effects. There had already been a review in 1940 of the disposition of Allied capital ships throughout all theatres of war. The most urgent need was for protection in the British home waters, followed by convoy duty in the Atlantic and Mediterranean operations. The needs in the Indian and Pacific Oceans were secondary, mainly for the escort of troop ships from the Empire countries. The priority of protecting the phosphate trade from Nauru was certainly low on the list.

Australia's navy were already playing an active part in Europe but, as a direct result of the raider attacks on and around Nauru, HMAS *Sydney* and HMAS *Westralia* were hastily ordered to return to Australian waters. While this helped to stop any further German raider activity in 1941, it removed two effective fighting ships from where they were really needed in Europe. It can be argued that those warships would have returned anyway, given the increasing likelihood of war in the Pacific with Japan, but strategists were clearly rattled by the raiders' success and did not want to chance a repetition. Australia's warships acted as escorts for phosphate ships around Nauru and Ocean Island and for newly introduced convoys across the Tasman Sea.

As noted in Chapter 9, another by-product of the raider attacks was the defensive arming of some of the outlying islands in their mandated territories, including Nauru and Ocean Islands. This was in defiance of the Treaty of Versailles, but justified at the time, because Japan was clearly breaching their treaty terms in the Caroline and Marshall Islands. Originally there were plans for two six-inch guns on each island but these were never installed because of shortage of equipment. Each island received only two small field guns which were later withdrawn when the war with Japan became unavoidable. It was obvious to the Allied military strategists that New Guinea and its outlying islands could not be defended against a Japanese invasion.

Security in New Zealand

The 1941 inquiry heard evidence on many of the day-to-day wartime operations in New Zealand. Eyssen's all-knowing bluster resulted in many seemingly benign procedures to be analysed to prevent shipping information being released either intentionally or inadvertently. The inquiry tackled the issues by stating that two conditions needed to be satisfied for secret information to be leaked: the information needed to be available, and it needed to be conveyable to the enemy.

On the first question of how secret information might become available, witnesses to the inquiry relayed many tales of gross complacency. While Britain maintained a high-profile 'Loose talk costs lives' propaganda campaign, people in New Zealand were accused of committing so many indiscretions that they were not taking the war seriously. The Controller of Censorship gave examples of family airmail letters which had to be redacted because they gave the name, sailing dates and destinations of troopships. Similarly, all radio messages had to be approved and the Censor was amazed at how many had to be refused because they included details of ship movements. The Police said in evidence that they had investigated many incidents of loose talk, particularly in pubs. Even some of the commodity suppliers and shipowners came in for criticism for thoughtlessness in preparing shipping schedules and for lack of security on the wharves. The inquiry heard stories of schedules lying around on office desks and readily given to anyone with a half-plausible excuse to be in a restricted area. The Railway Department was criticised for complacency by continuing the peace time practice of chalking the name of ships on the destination cards on the back of railway wagons for anyone to see. The inquiry went as far as questioning the reliability and discretion of office clerks who had access to sensitive material, suggesting a more formal security screening and 'need-to-know' allocation of work. The general conclusion was that nobody should be surprised if sensitive information was finding its way into the wrong hands.

The question of how sensitive information, when acquired, could be passed to an enemy was more difficult to address. The problem was that there had been no proven cases. The inquiry took evidence on the two main themes of illicit radio transmissions and coded messages in commercial messages and in the media.

All radio transmitters had to be licensed and the user security-checked. Nobody classified as an alien was allowed to possess or use a transmitter. Even doctors and hospitals using diathermy equipment for deep-heat treatment required a license, because the equipment needed little modification to be used as a transmitter. The inquiry heard how radio transmissions were monitored, not just by the authorities, but also by amateur listeners who reported any suspicious messages to the police. Overall, there was no evidence to suggest illegal radio use, but the inquiry recommended increased levels of vigilance. It was suggested that suspicions of mis-use could not be dismissed merely because no such instances had yet been detected.

The biggest concern in submissions by the public to the inquiry was in connection with national radio broadcasts and newspapers. There were many suggestions that dedications for birthdays, anniversaries, etc., could contain hidden code. Similarly, it was the practice for the public to ask for help in finding lost pets, missing cars or to announce local events. Again, nothing could be proved to the inquiry, but the scope for broadcasting or publishing coded messages was real. New rules were introduced which stopped announcements from the public and substantially increased the level of pre-recording and censorship.

The whole of the raider incident and the subsequent official inquiry gave the New Zealand government and public a big wake-up call. The war had arrived on their doorstep, yet there had been a general level of complacency and unwillingness to change pre-war attitudes. New procedures were quickly implemented to minimise the security risk, including a significant change in attitude towards the classification and internment of aliens. Once again, Captain Eyssen's bluster about his sources of information destroyed whatever intelligence opportunities there may have been. Had he simply told his captives the truth, that *Rangitane* was encountered fortuitously, New Zealand may have continued its lax attitude to security, to Germany's and Japan's advantage.

The end of a story is never really the end. People and places survive and it is interesting to see what became of the main players in the *Rangitane* Riddle.

Robert Eyssen and *Komet*

After destroying the phosphate installation at Nauru, *Komet* sailed to her new operational area in the Indian Ocean, changing her profile and adopting the Japanese name *Ryoku Maru*. Eyssen knew that his colleagues on *Atlantis* and *Pinguin* had had rich pickings in the Indian Ocean and he wanted to improve his sinking tally. The reality was that Eyssen had been at sea for six months and he had not made a single capture by himself. But despite his lack of success and the criticism by German naval control for releasing his prisoners and for attacking Nauru, Eyssen was promoted on 1 January, 1941 to Rear-Admiral, to become the highest ranking officer in the German merchant raider fleet.

Eyssen was to be thwarted in his ambitions in the Indian Ocean: he was ordered to turn south and to look for whaling ships off Antarctica. The only ships he found were Japanese and he learnt from them that he was more likely to find potential victims anchored at the Kerguelen Islands, further west in the southern Indian Ocean. Unfortunately for Eyssen the area was deserted and the paucity of victims continued to prey on his mind. There was to be little respite; in July he was ordered by naval command to return to Germany by October to have *Komet* refitted in readiness for a second tour.

In August, Eyssen finally had three kills to himself in quick succession near the Galapagos Islands, the first for thirteen months. But the improvement in morale was short lived; *Komet* had to re-provision and start her journey home, finally arriving at Hamburg on 30 November, after surviving a number of air attacks while running the gauntlet of the English Channel. She had been on patrol for an amazing 516 days, sailing 87,000 miles, but with only modest results in comparison with other raiders.

Komet was completely refitted with new armaments and welcomed her new commander, Ulrich Brochsien, in February 1942. His first task was to put *Komet* and her new crew through sea trials and gunnery training which was carried out in the Baltic during June and July. By September she was in Kiel to provision in readiness to break out to the Atlantic via the English Channel. But the British knew from Enigma intercepts and aerial photography that she was preparing to sail, and had followed her move from Kiel to Swindemunde and on to Flushing in Holland where she met minesweepers to escort her to the Atlantic. The Admiralty deployed destroyers and motor torpedo boats to be ready for *Komet* but she managed to escape serious engagement and reached Dunkirk and then Le Havre to start the final leg of her journey to open sea on 13 October. The Admiralty set Operation Bowery into effect, throwing nine destroyers, twelve motor torpedo boats and air reconnaissance into the search for *Komet* off Cape Barfleur. She and her escorts were sighted by an RAF *Swordfish* in the early hours of 14 October and a somewhat chaotic battle ensued. *Komet* was trapped and, despite orders to divert into Cherbourg, Captain

Brochsien continued a westerly course to the Atlantic. How she was hit is in dispute: a motor torpedo boat claimed a direct torpedo hit while others said that it was from shell fire. Either way, *Komet* exploded in a massive fireball which could be seen from the Channel Islands, forty miles away. All 351 crew perished. It is known that only two of her officers were from the original *Komet* but inevitably some of the other original crew must have died as well.

The remains of *Komet* lay undiscovered until 2007 when a diving enthusiast, Innes McCartney, researched her sinking and found her in separate halves. He remarked that he had seen many ships sunk by catastrophic explosion, but *Komet*'s disintegration was exceptional. She had been the smallest of all German merchant cruisers and was converted from a merchant ship with little of the hull strength of a warship. It is clear that her fully loaded arsenal had received a direct hit and she exploded into oblivion.

Rear Admiral Robert Eyssen had left *Komet* to become a naval liaison officer in Russia in 1942, later appointed as the head of the naval depot in Oslo. From there he became commander of the Third Military District in Vienna from which he retired in April 1945, just nine days before the end of the war in Europe. Eyssen published his war memoirs in 1960, dying the same year in Baden Baden.

Many of *Rangitane*'s prisoners referred to Eyssen as being pompous and full of himself, but he was clearly from the 'old school' of professional navy men. Despite his strategic blunders, Eyssen will be remembered for his humanity. How much he was influenced by Lionel Upton, we shall never know.

Kurt Weyher and *Orion*

When *Orion* left Emirau with her prisoners, she headed for Lamotrek to meet *Regensburg, Ole Jacob* and *Ermland*, three raider supply ships which had themselves been re-provisioned in Japan. *Orion's* boilers and engines were in desperate need of overhaul, which was started in the remote surroundings of Lamotrek. German naval command heard about the rescue of the Emirau survivors and concluded that the secrecy of both Lamotrek and Ailinglaplap had probably been compromised. Weyher decided to head for Maug to complete the refit, but he first transferred his remaining prisoners to *Ermland* which was to make her way back to Germany.

Orion's engines were serviced at Maug and on 5 February she set off with *Ole Jacob* in support to patrol the eastern Indian Ocean. Weyher was to have as little success as Eyssen in the following months. *Orion* travelled westwards towards the Seychelles and on to Madagascar, finally rounding the Cape in July. On the few occasions a ship was seen, it was usually from a neutral country but in one instance it was HMS *Cornwall* which had only recently sunk another raider, *Pinguin*. Weyher said that he was so lucky to have escaped without being seen.

Orion's progress was continually hampered by breakdowns, worn bearings and the incessant need for work on her engines. She consumed far too much fuel and needed frequent replenishment from supply ships. *Orion* and her crew were equally exhausted and Weyher was finally instructed to head for Bordeaux.

On the way home Weyher found a final victim: the SS *Chaucer* was on her way under ballast from Middlesbrough to Buenos Aires and, when challenged, put up a fight with her limited armaments. It took a total of ten torpedoes, many of which failed to explode, and over 400 shells to despatch *Chaucer*. Unfortunately the gun fire from the 5.9-inch guns shook *Orion*'s hull, and bolts sheared on the drive shaft mountings. She was in danger of shaking herself to pieces just as she was on the home run. She was escorted by submarines, destroyers and a minesweeper for the last lap into the Gironde estuary, and up to Bordeaux. As she drew up to her mooring on 23 August, 1941 she could see that the *Regensburg*, *Ole Jacob* and *Ermland* had all arrived safely in Bordeaux.

Orion had been 511 days at sea, just five fewer than *Komet*, but had sailed considerably further at 127,000 miles. During that time she had ten changes of disguise and name. It was clear that she could not be refitted for a second tour, so *Orion* was taken out of merchant raider service. Her armaments were removed and she became a repair ship until re-armed and re-named in 1943 as the *Hektor*, a gunnery training ship based in the Baltic. In early 1945 she reverted to her previous *Orion* name and was to have gone back into service as an armed merchant cruiser under the overall command of Bernhard Rogge, the former commander of *Atlantis*. But the war in northern Europe was nearing its climax and *Orion* was commandeered to evacuate military personnel and civilians fleeing from the Russian advance through East Prussia. She carried 20,000 evacuees over sixteen round trips from the eastern Baltic ports, to relative safety, incurring only minimal damage. But on May 4, 1945, just a few days before Germany surrendered, *Orion* went to the aid of survivors from the battleship *Schlesien,* which had struck a mine near Swinemunde. She was attacked by Russian fighter bombers and was gutted by fire, killing over 150 of her crew. *Orion* was beached and gradually broken up in the post-war years.

Kurt Weyher, *Orion*'s previous commander, was transferred to the Baltic in 1941 and held chief of operations posts in the Eastern Mediterranean, Adriatic, Aegean and Black Sea. In 1944 he became chief of staff of the Romanian navy and finally commander-in-chief and rear-admiral in East Fresia. He was taken into captivity by the Allied powers in July 1945, claiming that he had the distinction of surrendering in one war as the

Kaiser's youngest cadet and in another war as Hitler's youngest admiral.

The Royal Navy had the job of disarming and controlling what remained of the *Kriegsmarine* ships, shore installations, and the tens of thousands of personnel who had surrendered. The British had learnt lessons from the aftermath of the First World War when uncertainty and discontent among the defeated Germans led to them scuttling their Grand Fleet at Scapa Flow. This time the Royal Navy involved the senior German navy officers and the existing *Kriegsmarine* command structure to organise and manage the upkeep of ships, infrastructure and personnel. One of the most senior officers was Kurt Weyher who, together with Vice Admiral Zieb, was described by the British commander-in-chief as a willing and reliable partner. As has been previously noted in Chapter 5, Weyher had witnessed at first hand the collapse of discipline, sabotage and eventual mutiny of many naval personnel in 1918 and the conditions were ripe for history to be repeated. It is clear that Weyher was genuinely honour-bound to help the British to maintain order and to co-operate in the handover of the war machine. Weyher and Zieb are reported to have taken personal control of the remaining warships at Wilhelmshaven until their disposal under the Potsdam Agreement had been finalised. There was an undercurrent of dissent because some of the warships were to be handed over to Russia as part of the disarmament and reparation arrangements. Weyher and Zieb had to ensure that any signs of subversion and sabotage were quickly suppressed.

Following Weyher's release in 1947, he worked as a ship chandler and in 1961 became a political writer and lecturer on military science. He died on 17 December, 1991 at the age of 90. Weyher's son, Hein-Peter, followed in his father's respected footsteps, rising to the highest ranks in the post-war German navy.

Kurt Weyher was extremely popular with his fellow officers and crew on *Orion*. He was often described as a no-nonsense disciplinarian but with a wicked sense of humour. Being much younger than Robert Eyssen, he may have reflected a different era or culture in the German navy, possibly manifesting itself in the disagreements he often had with Eyssen. His position over the release of the prisoners is totally justified from a strategic point of view, but this should not detract from his overall humane treatment of his captives.

Captain Lionel Upton

After the survivors' celebrations finished in Sydney, Lionel Upton was asked to travel to New Zealand to give evidence to the Commission of Inquiry which sat in February and March, 1941. Upton had clearly lost much weight during his imprisonment; one of *Rangitane*'s passengers described him as 'sparse' and another thought that he was seriously ill.

Upton's evidence at the inquiry was at times rambled and confused. He was recalled towards the end of the inquiry to clarify a number of conflicting statements, but he was treated with respect and understanding in the light of what he had endured. He was finally released and arrived in Liverpool on 22 May, spending most of the summer of 1941 on leave in Hove, during which time he made a broadcast on the BBC describing his exploits. In June he received a postcard from Robert Potts, one of *Rangitane*'s stewards, who had been transported back to Germany and was in a prisoner-of-war camp. Potts wanted to let Upton know that everybody except James Adams had arrived safely in Germany and that they were being well-treated.

Being a naval reservist, Upton knew that it was to have been his last trip in command of *Rangitane* before being called up for naval duty. While it is questionable whether Upton was too old or, indeed, too unwell, to return to sea on naval duty, the fact that he had signed the parole agreement precluded him from anything other than a shore appointment. In September, 1941 Upton was assigned to HMS *President* which was permanently moored on the Thames, working in the trade division on the relatively benign task of equipment inspection. Cecille Edgeley, the daughter of one of his neighbours in Hove, remembers him going off to catch the train to London every morning, smartly dressed in his naval uniform, always with a cigarette in his hand. Cecille was a Wren and had known Upton since she was a child. Whenever she met him, and they were both in uniform, they theatrically saluted each other in fits of giggles.

Upton was released from the navy in December, 1945 and, at nearly sixty years old, described himself as 'retired and unemployed.' Although he was still on the reserve list, it was the first time since his younger schooldays that he had no connection with the sea; even at fourteen years old, Upton had studied seamanship at Holyrood School in Bognor which had a Royal Naval Academy. He clearly missed his naval connections: he periodically advised the Admiralty that he was fit for service and 'would be a volunteer for early recall.' In 1948 he started a private car hire and driving school which continued until he reached retirement age. Upton was finally taken off the reserve list when he was sixty-eight years old. A local butcher's boy recalls delivering meat on his bicycle to Upton, describing him as tall and gaunt. 'He sat by his fireplace which had polished brass shell cases on each side. He would keep his cigarette butts and roll them into new cigarettes.' His neighbour, Cecille Edgeley says that her father and Upton were good friends, describing him as 'down-to-earth, never enough money and that the family were genuine, honourable people.'

Lionel Upton died on 28 October, 1970 aged eighty-four. Like Robert Eyssen, Upton was clearly from the 'old school' of professional seamen and this was to his distinct advantage when negotiating with Eyssen over the release of the prisoners. How much influence Upton had will never be known. He was obviously not a wily old sea dog; he simply took control of a desperate situation without issue. His evident emotion in his speeches and great humanity when writing the dozens of letters of thanks to his saviours leave the impression of a straightforward seaman who rose to the challenge with distinction.

The Stuarts

Judge Stuart was on *Rangitane* because he had been sacked from his post as Chief Justice of Tonga. He was on his way with his wife to take up his new appointment as Second Puisne Judge in British Guiana. His version was that his new appointment was because of his good work in Tonga; the reality was that Stuart and his wife had crossed swords with too many people in Tonga, particularly Queen Salote. He was described as confrontational and garrulous with ideas above his station. In her book on Queen Salote, Elizabeth Wood-Ellem said that Stuart thought he saw maladministration, corruption and subversion everywhere, and set out to expose it. While some abuse did exist, he went too far. He was tireless in reporting alleged misdemeanours of his close working colleagues and tried to bully Queen Salote to set up formal inquiries. Many of the Stuarts' actions were motivated by revenge: they believed that they should have had a social status closer to the royal family. Anybody who did get close to the queen, or disagreed with them, became the focus of the Stuarts' intimidation. By the time they were removed from Tonga and had boarded *Rangitane*, they were well practised in vindictiveness.

An alternative title of this book could have been 'Who was the real enemy?' and the answer might have been 'The Stuarts.' While both Stuarts were obviously intelligent and highly educated, it is amazing that they did not put their education, experience and status to far better use after *Rangitane*'s capture. In Judge Stuart's position, he could have stepped up to the mark and, with Captain Upton, have represented the prisoners in dealings with the Germans. Starr Stuart was a fluent German speaker, yet there are no records of her talking to the captors. One would have thought that, as a minimum, they could have shown by example, how to deal with such a sensitive situation.

They chose however, to make enemies of their own countrymen instead of their captors. Once again, Stuart saw treason amongst his fellow prisoners and was vocal in his suspicions. During his first day of captivity, Stuart was incensed that a RNZAF search plane had not spotted the raiders and was convinced that the pilot was a subversive and 'should be placed under control for the duration of the war.' Similarly, he was going to have one of the *Holmwood* crewmen imprisoned because he believed him 'to be a communist sympathiser.'

The most disturbing aspect of the Stuarts' behaviour was the way they treated the female CORB escorts. What started the hatred is unknown, but it was reciprocated and continued long after they were released. The Germans were obviously bemused by the bad relationship: as noted in Chapter 5, Stuart was told that if Germans could respect and honour British women, then he certainly should. The Stuarts later claimed that everybody had been atrociously treated by their captors. As has already been shown, this was nonsense. Margaret Osborne summed up the Stuarts succinctly: 'In their position, they could have been such an example and help to us instead of making us ashamed to be their fellow prisoners.'

When he was finally released from captivity, Stuart made many allegations, all non-specific. His accusations to both the intelligence services and the press were bluster. Unfortunately, he used his position as 'a high judicial officer' to demand investigation and he was a significant influence in the government's decision to set up a commission of inquiry. It is disappointing that the Stuarts did not appear as witnesses. The sight of Judge Stuart, with his self-perceived status and crusade against anybody who disagreed with him, being cross-examined by other equally qualified 'high judicial officials' would have been explosive.

Not long after, the Tongans received an unwelcome reminder of their departed Chief Justice: he submitted a claim to Tonga for compensation for the loss of personal effects on *Rangitane*.

After two years in British Guiana, Stuart was appointed Puisne Judge in Dar es Salaam, Tanganyika. This probably suited him because Tanganyika was part of the former colony of German East Africa and was another German possession mandated to the British as reparation after the First World War. Starr Stuart died suddenly in London in June 1944, but Judge Stuart re-married and continued working until his retirement in 1948. He died in 1967, in South Africa, his birthplace.

Emirau Island

After *Nellore* departed with the last of the survivors, Emirau Island returned temporarily to its quiet existence. The arrival of 496 people had stretched the meagre resources to the limit. The Cook and Collett families submitted claims to the government for the replacement of food and equipment, particularly for the repair to the truck that Cook said had been damaged by the Germans when transporting meat carcasses to their ships. They received a number of letters from government agencies thanking them for their forbearance, in particular a letter from Prime Minister Fraser. But it was a letter from Captain Upton and his fellow captains which was most welcome: they learnt that the survivors had made a collection and had raised sufficient money to buy two powerful electricity generators for the island and also money for the local inhabitants who had donated their garden produce.

Life in 1941 returned to normal but the omens were not good: although Japan had not yet entered the war, their reconnaissance aircraft were creeping closer to New Guinea and contingency plans were made to evacuate Emirau when hostilities broke out. Mrs Cook and Mrs Collett returned to Australia. In January, 1942 the Japanese started their invasion, bombing nearby Kavieng and Rabaul. Pastor Atkins, the Director of the Seventh-Day Adventists in New Guinea based on Emirau's neighbouring island of Mussau had hidden their mission boat and, on a signal from Trevor Collett, sailed to Emirau to rescue the few remaining inhabitants. They set out for Rabaul, over 200 miles away, sailing at night and hiding by day but on final approach they found that it had fallen to the Japanese. Over the following days they joined up with others trying to flee, but Pastor Atkins became ill and, deteriorating rapidly, insisted that he should be left behind as he was hindering their escape. Trevor Collett decided to stay with Atkins and both were captured and imprisoned in Rabaul, where Pastor Atkins died.

The Japanese occupied many of the New Guinea islands, but only established an observation post on Emirau. The main stronghold in the area was at Kavieng, just seventy miles away which had become a major staging point for aircraft flying from the Japanese island of Truk, to Rabaul, their new military administration centre. Early in 1943, the American forces under General MacArthur identified the capture of Kavieng as an essential part of the fight against the Japanese but it was to be another year before action could be taken. It was during this time that the Australian authorities sought the help of Carl Leopold Bruno Wilde at his home in Sydney. Having spent the happiest years of his life with Juanita on Emirau, he knew more about the island and its surrounding shoreline than anybody. Wilde had suffered the indignity of having been detained as an enemy alien at the Loveday internment camp and his health began to fail. This was a man who had arrived in New Guinea and had become a most successful frontiersman, establishing first a coca business on Emirau, then a coffee plantation at Wau. His son-in-law negotiated his release and accepted responsibility for Wilde. When John Meehan wrote a short biography of Wilde he commented

> This same enemy alien was contacted by the Allied Intelligence Bureau for help; the US Forces were to land on Emirau Island in March 1944, and the planners had very little

information available. Wilde was able to provide very useful details about the reefs, anchorages, water depths, etc.

The Americans had decided to re-take Emirau and use it as a springboard for their assault on Kavieng and Rabaul. They gave Emirau the codename Beefsteak, and on 20 March, 1994 their Marines invaded with no enemy opposition. By nightfall there were over 3,700 troops camping on the island, with 800 tons of supplies and equipment. Within a month there were 18,000 men and 4,000 tons of supplies. Construction battalions started building two heavy bomber air strips using local crushed stone. Within just a few months, there was sufficient infrastructure to accommodate 210 fighters and 84 heavy bombers, together with port facilities for capital ships. Emirau had become a huge garrison which supported the fight against the Japanese.

When the marines began their offensive against Kavieng and Rabaul, there were horrendous recriminations by the Japanese against the Allied prisoners and civilians. On Kavieng wharf there was a mass execution, for which the perpetrators were tried at a war crimes tribunal and executed after the war. At Rabaul, Trevor Collett from Emirau was one of 1,053 civilians and Australian soldiers who were transferred from internment camp to the *Montevideo Maru*, a Japanese merchant ship, for transfer to Japan for forced labour. She was sighted and torpedoed by the American submarine USS *Sturgeon*. Trevor Collett and all but eighteen crew members perished.

The American marines handed control of the Emirau garrison to the Australian army in September 1944 and the Royal New Zealand Air Force took charge in December. In July, 1945 attempts were made to dispose of dozens of vehicles, aircraft, spare parts and the general detritus of an occupying force. Most of it was pushed off the high cliffs into the sea before all personnel were finally withdrawn.

Emirau was unrecognisable to its returning inhabitants. Since the war only a scattering of small village encampments have been maintained by natives living under subsistence conditions. A comparison of Emirau today with how it was ninety years earlier under Carl Wilde's management shows how a society can grow, then wane. For many years, there has been a Seventh-Day Adventist church presence on Emirau, which binds the community together. When Rod Leonard, a charter plane operator in Australia, visited the island in 2010, he was appalled to find the population in such poor condition, despite being surrounded by a sea teeming with shellfish and a land capable of sustaining protein-bearing meat, all potential food which is banned by the local church doctrine.

The American-built airstrips and service roads still exist but there is little sign of Wilde's homestead. The monument to his wife, Juanita, still stands and is maintained in pristine condition by the local inhabitants. In 1977, the Australian destroyer RANS *Torrens* visited Emirau and another monument was erected to acknowledge the part played by the island in the fight against Japan.

Orion's prisoners

Orion left Emirau with eighty-five of *Rangitane*'s passengers and crew and ninety-eight from other ships whom Captain Weyher had refused to release. One of them was Father Ball, a CORB escort, who originally was to have been released, but volunteered to travel with the remaining prisoners. A few days later at Lamotrek they were transferred to *Ermland*, another raider supply ship which had re-provisioned in Japan. She was heading for the Atlantic via Cape Horn to meet the *Admiral von Scheer* and finally to Bordeaux in France. *Orion*'s Captain Weyher described *Ermland* as 'a rat-infested rust bucket' and insisted that it was pressure washed before the prisoners were transferred.

In his personal account, Father Ball said that life on *Ermland* was more relaxed than on *Orion.* They had the run of the forward part of the ship for much of the day and were hardly bothered by the German crew, most of whom were merchant mariners. The stores were clearly Japanese and he even complained that the food was starchy; after everybody had lost weight over the previous month, he said that many showed the signs of stomach paunches. In March, Father Ball had the sad task of conducting a funeral service for James Adams, *Rangitane*'s chief steward. For some time Adams had been 'hopelessly ill, having been deprived of the liquor on which he had previously depended.'

Frank Ellison, a *Rangitane* steward, remembers that life during the day was much better on *Ermland* but that he dreaded the evenings when some of the men could become very unpleasant. He said that another steward, James Houligan, entertained the prisoners with his wonderful singing but that everyone thanked Frank, thinking that it was he who was the singer. This was ironic: only a few years later, when he joined a choir, he was advised to mime because he was tone deaf! The New Zealand air force recruits proved to be real characters, always chirpy and even produced an evening variety show using somewhat limited resources.

After meeting and collecting even more prisoners from the *Admiral von Scheer* in the Atlantic, *Ermland* reached Bordeaux on 4 April, 1941. The prisoners were transferred to a POW transit camp near St. Medard-en-Jalles and then by train to Stalag XB POW camp near Sandbostel in north-west Germany. What they found there was horrific: while the British and Allied seamen were housed in barely humane conditions in one part of the camp, another section housed Serbians and Russian prisoners and a third part was for civilians and 'undesirables'. Frank Ellison said that the two other sections defied belief.

In late 1941 a new camp, Marlag und Milag Nord, was built at Westertimke near Bremen. The Marlag section held Royal

Navy seamen while Milag held merchant seamen. Both sections were under the control of *Kriegsmarine* personnel and the prisoners settled down to a relatively organised life dominated by the irregular arrival of Red Cross parcels.

Unfortunately, *Rangitane*'s RNZAF recruits, being enlisted military personnel, were sent to a number of different prisoner-of-war camps including Dulag Luft, the notorious Stalag VIIIB at Lamsdorf (now in Poland), Stalag Luft III at Sagan (also now in Poland) and Stalag Luft VI at Heydekrug (now in Lithuania).

Others

Some other *Rangitane* survivors suffered unpleasant fates. Sixty-eight year old Chief Steward Henry Anker was released from POW camp on medical grounds and returned to England to live with his wife in Wimbledon. On the night of 22 July, 1944 he and his wife Frances were killed by a stray bomb on their house. CORB escort Annie (Nan) Willis returned to England and later joined the Queen Alexandra's Imperial Military Nursing Service. She was on the SS *Khedive Ismail*, a troopship in convoy with three others sailing from Mombasa to Colombo. On board were 1,511 people including eighty-three women, mainly nurses. Only 208 men and six women survived when a Japanese submarine torpedoed the ship, which sank in under two minutes. Nan Willis had survived her *Rangitane* ordeal but perished on *Khedive Ismail*.

Some of *Rangitane*'s other CORB escorts received surprisingly insensitive treatment by the Government. After arriving in Sydney they were given a short time to take a ship back to England, otherwise they would not receive any subsistence and would have to pay for their own passage home. Two of the badly wounded escorts, Phyllis Matthews and Florence Mundie, asked the Government for financial help because the seriousness of their injuries prevented them from working. Neither was successful. The Reverend Emlyn Davies, husband of CORB escort Elsie Davies who was killed on *Rangitane*, wrote to the Government 'Mrs. Davies death has meant my finding another person to attend to the household duties of my house' adding 'I naturally look to you to make compensation as shall be adequate for the deprivation involved.' Again, the claim was unsuccessful.

Appendix: *Rangitane* crew and passengers

Died

Name		Home town	Affiliation
Adams	James	Girvan	Crew
Beeston	Miss Doris Anne	Grange, S. Australia	CORB
de Castella	Mrs Catherine M	Chiswick	Crew
Davies	Mrs Elsie Mae	North Finchlay	CORB
Dixon	James Yeomans	Wellington, NZ	CORB
Handley	Daniel		Crew
Herbert-Jones	Miss Elinor E	Montgomeryshire	CORB
McNulty	James Gerard		Crew
Moore	William James		Crew
Pithers	Francis C	Gillingham	Crew
Ray	Charles	Romford	Crew
Scott	Miss Alice Una	Aylesbury	CORB
Skinner	Miss Jessie Ann		Crew
Strickfuss	Frederick	Canning Town	Crew
Strickfuss	Samuel H	Canning Town	Crew
Tocher	Andrew	Ayton, Berwickshire	CORB

Crew released on Emirau

Name		Date of birth	Job
Almond	John W (Jack)	10/09/1918	3rd Electrician
Ashcroft	W		Assistant Steward
Balding	Jessie (Janie)		Stewardess
Barley	Geoffrey	13/02/1918	Seventh Engineer
Becker	A		Linen steward
Bell	L		Assistant Steward
Bowering	R E		Greaser
Brabbins	Douglas Victor		Assistant Steward
Bryan	W		Assistant Steward
Burn	W		BR/Assist Steward
Cameron	Edward A	26/12/1916	Sixth Engineer
Cannan	E		Assistant Storekeeper
Carpenter	Cecil Edward		Writer
Carrothers	Charles		Deck Electrician
Claridge	Joseph	05/04/1916	Assistant Steward
Clarke	Sid		Writer
Clint	Francis G (Bobby)		Assistant Steward
Collison	William	15/02/1908	Tourist Steward
Colwell	John M	09/10/1913	Third Engineer
Cooke	J	28/06/1904	Greaser
Corcoran	J		OS
Courtney	W		Assistant Steward
Cowan	R	03/06/1915	Assistant Steward
Cox	Albert Thomas	06/07/1894	Chief Engineer
Crawford	Dr J	18/06/1873	Ship's Surgeon
Crogan	J		Assistant Steward
Cunningham	P		Assistant Steward
Cuthbertson	James T R		Assistant Steward
Dean	C		Pantryman

Dixson	Albert	09/09/1893	Assistant Steward
Dowsett	Albert		BR/Assist Steward
Dye	John	01/09/1892	Pantryman
Eaglestone	L		Cook
Edgar	Thomas J	05/09/1901	Second Engineer
Edwards	J		Printer
Evans	E		BR/Assist Steward
Evans	W	29/03/1897	Assistant Steward
Fanning	P	16/08/1887	AB
Findlay	R		Refrigerating Greaser
Finn	J		Stewards boy
Forster	T	19/01/1896	Assistant Steward
Francis	William		Ship's Cook
Galloway	G		Assistant Cook
Gellatly	C		Assistant Steward
Glew	S		Tourist baths
Gray	P E	17/06/1920	Assistant Steward
Griffin	A		AB
Griffin	Frank A	08/12/1917	Eighth Engineer
Groombridge	E	25/03/1916	Tourist baths
Hales	J		Second Baker
Hall	J J		Sculleryman
Hallett	Norman James	11/08/1910	First Radio Officer
Hamilton	H		Assistant Steward
Hankin	S	01/12/1922	Stewards boy
Hardacre	George		Tourist baths
Harries	Miss C		Nursing sister
Harrington	F		Deck Crew
Harris	P		Saloon steward
Hayes	J		Nightwatchman
Heels	A		BR/Assist Steward

Henderson	Clarence John		Assistant Steward
Hodgson	T S	04/08/1914	Fourth Engineer
Hogarth	Eric		Greaser
Hogg	W	01/01/1911	Fireman
Hopkins	Ernest Hamler	16/04/1899	Chief Officer
Howells	Frederick		Chief Butcher
Hughes	T		AB
Hunt	James (Jim)		Steward
Hutchinson	P	06/06/1884	Greaser
Jarvis	Mr R G	24/05/1906	DBS ex Rangitata
Jefferey	Norman		Assistant Steward
Jenkins	A		Assistant Steward
Jenner	W		AB
Johnston	John	26/11/1907	Chief Elect Engineer
Kavanagh	J	10/05/1914	Assistant Steward
Kerr	H	04/05/1894	Pantryman
Kingsford	Fred		OS
Lacey	T		Nightwatchman
Lawrence	W		1st class Barman
Mackay	Donald		AB
Macrae	Alexander	13/10/1875	Chief Refrig Engineer
Mahoney	J	09/06/1911	Third Butcher
Mannington	Miss P		Stewardess
Maynard	Charles Spencer		AB
McCarthy	J		Assistant Steward
McCristall	F		Assistant Steward
McLean	William	21/09/1911	Second Refrig Engineer
McMahon	B		Storekeeper
McMurray	P		Assistant Steward
Miles	Fred	16/06/1904	AB
Mills	A		Assistant Steward

Moore	Reg		Smoke room Steward
Muller	T	31/01/1921	Assistant Steward
Nobbs	John W	03/07/1921	OS
Norman	G N	19/08/1911	Third Radio Officer
Normington	John Robert	28/10/1906	Tenth Engineer
Norrington	F		Tourist Steward
Norton	A		Tourist baths
Nottley	W		Assistant Steward
Pegler	John		Assistant Steward
Penman	J	13/08/1913	Fifth Engineer
Perry	Mrs G		Stewardess
Phillips	Edward M		Quartermaster
Plumb	Mrs Elizabeth Anne		First Class Stewardess
Poole	Cyril David Roy	14/05/1913	Third Mate
Porter	J		Stewards boy
Price	Haydn		Assistant Steward
Pritchard	G (T?)		Assistant Steward
Pybis	F		Greaser
Ragg	M		Fireman
Rees	Frank		Quartermaster
Reid	Charles D	17/11/1915	Ninth Engineer
Reilly	J	05/08/1889	AB
Riome	A		BR/Assist Steward
Robins	B		Assistant Steward
Robinson	H	23/11/1910	Bos'uns Mate
Rogers	F	18/10/1902	Assistant Steward
Rowe	J		Refrigerating greaser
Sheehan	J		Assistant Steward
Sinclair	Donald Bain	28/01/1908	Second Electrician
Small	W		Assistant Steward
Smillie	S G		BR/Assist Steward

Smith	T	13/02/1895	Assistant Steward
Snowden	John Philip		Deck Crew Plumber
Sowerby	Leo Graham		Assistant Steward
Stewart	W M	02/11/1917	Eleventh Engineer
Summers	A		Deck Steward
Tasker	D		BR/Assist Steward
Taylor	Robin Gordon	31/05/1919	Fourth Officer
Thorpe	R		Sculleryman
Upton	Herbert Lionel	22/05/1886	Captain
Vallerie	L		Quartermaster
Vanner	V	10/01/1909	Hospital attendant
Walker	John Robert	18/11/1900	Deck Mechanic
Ward	F W	17/09/1901	Second Radio Officer
Watkins	Reginald		OS
White	J		Assistant Steward
Williams	Henry Stewart	18/11/1898	Second Mate
Wilson	George W I	03/01/1916	RNVR/gunlayer
Windridge	Donald F	25/05/1913	AB/ RN gunner
Winn	R		Quartermaster
Woods	J		BR/Assist Steward
Young	H		Quartermaster
Zerface	Peter Philip		Barber

Passengers released on Emirau

Name		Date of birth	Affiliation
Alston	Miss Cristianne		CORB
Black	Miss Mary (Molly)	15/01/1910	Passenger
Bolenski	Mr Julian	07/03/1918	Batory
Borkowska	Miss S Albina		Batory
Cameron	A	09/12/1889	Baltannic
Child	Miss Florence Kate		CORB
Clothier	Mrs Annabelle (Ella)		CORB
Conolly	Cyril Robert (Bob)	10/12/2011	Baltannic
Czajkowski	Mr Waclaw		Batory
da Costa	Miss Eileen Louise		CORB
Daramoniec (Korek)	Mrs J		Batory
Dunsmuir	Miss Mary Ewing		CORB
Edge	Geraldine		CORB
Engel	Mr Josef		Batory
Fagan	F		Baltannic
Golding	Sister Rosalie Edith		CORB
Gorecka(Marcs)	Miss M		Batory
Haworth	Mr Ashley A	10/04/1918	NZ Fleet Air Arm
Hooper	Mr Thomas Alva	10/09/1920	NZ Fleet Air Arm
Jackson	F	01/09/1905	Baltannic
Jastrzybski	J		Batory
Jefferey	Mrs Phyllis Joan Mary		Passenger
Kelly	Rev Father Denis		CORB
King	Mr J (Jack) A	18/04/1918	NZ Fleet Air Arm
King	Mr James R	20/07/1918	NZ Fleet Air Arm
Klos	Miss S Magdalena		Batory
Kofoed	Mr Albert Graham	19/02/1919	NZ Fleet Air Arm
Korak	Miss K Marta		Batory

Labanowicz	Miss L Anna		Batory
Lekadia	Miss Pilcek		Batory
Lorenc	Miss L Antonina		Batory
MacDonald	Flora		Passenger
Maslinska	Miss M Stanislaiva		Batory
Matthews	Miss Phyllis Maud		CORB
McComish	F		Baltannic
McLean	Miss K H		Passenger
MacLean	Mr Donald I N (Ian)	15/07/1918	NZ Fleet Air Arm
Menzies	William Halley Brown	04/08/1896	Baltannic
Millar	Mr Andrew Cleland	27/04/1919	NZ Fleet Air Arm
Mundie	Florence E. M.		CORB
Nawraccala	Mr Hieronim	13/09/1912	Batory
Newland	Tom S	14/08/1920	NZ Fleet Air Arm
Navarkowski	Mr Roman		Batory
Osborne	Miss Margaret E		CORB
Panton	Walter McG	09/10/1917	NZ Fleet Air Arm
Pearson	Miss Eleanor Mary		CORB
Podgorska	Miss P Pelagia		Batory
Pratzerowa	Miss F Michelenia		Batory
Quenault	William		Baltannic
Roberts	Jack H	22/03/1917	NZ Fleet Air Arm
Sandbach	Betsy (Blanche)		CORB
Schmidt	Mr Richard O	07/11/1917	NZ Fleet Air Arm
Schneider	Mr Henryk	06/04/1923	Batory
Shaw	Harry	16/06/1924	Baltannic
Smith	Mr T		Baltannic
Stolecka	Miss S Helena		Batory
Stuart	Mr William H		Passenger
Stuart	Mrs Edith Starr		Passenger
Sutcliffe-Hey	Mrs M E M (Eileen)		CORB

Thomas	Mr J	02/04/1892	Baltannic
Tomczak	Miss T Maria		Batory
Trend	Mr D	27/03/1908	Baltannic
Voss	Mr Edward J	25/11/1919	NZ Fleet Air Arm
Wallis	Mr W	04/07/1911	Baltannic
Williams	Mr Arthur G Reeve	17/02/1920	NZ Fleet Air Arm
Willis	Miss Annie A (Nan)		CORB
Wilmowocz	Mr Jan	21/01/1921	Batory
Wilson	Mr H (Tug)	17/01/1919	Baltannic

Crew detained on *Orion*

Name		Date of birth	Job
Anker	Henry G		Chief Steward
Barker	Philip		Boatswain
Barnes	Henry		Second Cook
Bass	Leslie		Able Seaman
Bourgoing	Thomas William		Chief Cook
Cain	Alan		Deck Boy
Cheeseman	Alfred		Greaser
Ellison	Frank	13/07/1920	Assistant Steward
Francis	Thomas		Bosun mate
Gorman	James		Sailor
Greene	Albert		Steward
Hall	Frank		Able Seaman
Hanson	John		Asst Steward
Harrison	George		Steward
Healey	Timothy		Fireman
Henderson	John		Watchman/Gun crew
Hird	David		Steward

Houligan	James		Steward
Jefferson	Donovan		Steward
Kennedy	John		OS
Knight	Henry		Steward
Knowles	Reginald		Steward
Lake	George		Chief Baker
Lock	Keith Wlliam		Fireman
Lyng	James		Assistant Cook
Macdonald	Alexander		Lampman
Mason	Albert		Sailor
Maugham	Edward M		Purser
McBride	Douglas James (Jimmy)		Able Seaman
McDuff	John (Jack)		Sailor (Butcher?)
McLaughlin	John		Butcher
Moriarty	D		Assistant Steward
Parrott	William		Musician
Potts	Robert T		Assistant Steward
Pring	Christopher		Steward
Rouse	Walter		Pantryman
Scott	Kenneth		Steward
Scott	Malcolm		Carpenter
Shearing	Edgar		Steward
Smith	Ronlad F		Quartermaster
Stanford	Albert		Greaser
Stewart	John		Carpenter
Strickfuss	Stanley	16/11/1889	Donkeyman
Thompson	W (Johnny)		Galley boy
Turner	Edward		Steward
Wetherill	W		Assistant Steward
Woods	Peter		Barman
Woolacott	Reginald		Nightwatchman

Passengers detained on *Orion*

Name		Date of birth	Job
Allan	Peter D		Civilian
Ball	Rev Father Ernest R		CORB
Baryla	Bronislaw (Bruno)		Batory
Bieniaszczyk	Jan		Batory
Briggs	Frank C		
Brown	Wallace C (Brownie)		RNZ Air Force
Burn	Maxwell H		RNZ Air Force
Cookson	Harold		Baltannic
Corcoran	William		NZ Fleet Air Arm
Daley	William Albert (Bill)		RNZ Air Force
Dark	Jack H		NZ Fleet Air Arm
Dowding	Hector MacD (Mac)		NZ Fleet Air Arm
Dynarkowsky	Bruno		Batory
Fitzsimons	B G		
Fox	A R E (Bert)		RNZ Air Force
Garnett	Thomas		
Gough	Stanley		
Grajewski	Kazimierz		Batory
Grimes	Leslie		
Harden	Billy Noel		RNZAF Radar team
Hawkhead	Edward H L (Ted)		RNZ Air Force
Hayer	A E	24/11/1891	
Huggett	Brian M (Skin)		RNZ Air Force
Hunt	Frank I R		RNZ Air Force
Jones	Alan Fitzgerald (Spike)		RNZ Air Force
Kimberley	Harold M (Kim)		RNZAF Radar team
Lewis	Henry R (Chuck)	23/05/1916	RNZ Air Force
McDonald	Arthur George		RNZ Air Force
Murray	John Donald (Jack)		RNZ Air Force

Parker	Percy S	RAF Corporal
Shearer	Keith William	RNZ Air Force
Smith	John	Baltannic
Sommerville	Geoffrey Field (Slim)	RNZ Air Force
Strawinski	N	Batory
Shaw	Ian James	RNZAF Radar team
Zawada	Max	Baltannic

Bibliography

Books

Andrade, Allan. *Leopoldville, a Tragedy Too Long Secret.* USA: Xlibris Corporation, 2009

Barker, Ralph. *Children of the Benares.* London: Grafton Books, 1990

Barley, Geoffrey. *Caught by a Nazi Raider.* London: New Zealand Shipping Company, 1941

Bauer, Friedrich L. *Decrypted Secrets.* Garching: Springer, 1997

Beesley, Patrick. *Very Special Intelligence.* London: Chatham Publishing, 2006

Bell, Les and Shadbolt, Gillian Heming. New South Wales: Rosenberg Publishing Pty. Ltd., 2002

Bennett, G. R. & R. *Survivors.* London: The Hambledon Press, 1999

Bird, Arthur H. *Farewell Milag.* East Sussex: British Red Cross Society, 1995

Brennecke, H. J. *Ghost Cruiser HK33.* London: William Kimber and Co. Ltd., 1954

Bridgland, Tony. *Sea Killers in Disguise.* Barnsley: Pen & Sword Books, 1999

Campbell, A. B. *Salute the Red Duster. London*: Christopher Johnson, 1952

Carr, J. Revell. *All Brave Sailors.* London: Hodder and Stoughton, 2004

Crabb, Brian James. *Passage to Destiny.* Stamford: Paul Watkins, 1997

Cowman, Mrs. Chas. E. *Streams in the Desert.* London: Oliphants Ltd., 1966

Cwiklinski, Jan. *The Captain Leaves his Ship.* New York: Doubleday & Company, 1955

Detmers, Theodor. *The Raider Kormoron.* London: William Kimber and Co. Ltd., 1959

Duffy, James P. *Hitler's Secret Pirate Fleet.* Nebraska: Greenwood Publishing Group Inc., 2005

Eyssen, Robert. *Komet. Jugenheim:* Koehlers Verlagsgesellschaft, 1960

Fenby, Jonathon. *The Sinking of Lancastria.* London: Simon & Schuster UK Ltd., 2005

Fethney, Michael. *The Absurd and the Brave.* Sussex: The Book Guild Ltd., 1990

Frank, Wolfgand and Rogge, Bernhard. *Under Ten Flags.* New York: Ballantine Books Inc., 1956

Geise, Otto and Wise, James. *Shooting the War.* Annapolis: Naval Institute Press, 2003

Gill, George Hermon. *Royal Australian Navy.* Canberra: Australian War Memorial, 1957

Hiery, Hermann Joseph. *The Neglected War.* Hawaii: University of Hawaii Press, 1995

Hinsley, F. H. And Stripp, Alan (Ed). *Code Breakers.* Oxford: Oxford University Press, 1993

Holman, Gordon. *In Wake of Endeavour.* London: Charles Knight, 1973

Hore, Peter. *Sydney Cipher and Search.* Suffolk: Seafarers Books, 2009

Hutching, Megan (Ed). *Inside Stories. New Zealand Prisoners of War Remember.* Auckland: Harper Collins, 2002

Inglis, Ruth. *The Children's War.* Great Britain: William Collins Sons & Co. Ltd., 1989

Jackson, Carlton. *Who Will Take Our Children?* London: Methuan London Ltd., 1985

Jones, Nigel. *The Birth of the Nazis.* London: John Murray (Publishers) Ltd., 1987

Jones, W. A. *Prisoner of the Kormoron.* Sydney: Australian Publishing Co. Pty. Ltd., 1944

Kahn, David. *The Codebreakers.* New York: Scribner, 1967

Kirk, Allan Alexander. *Fair Winds and Rough Seas*. Wellington, New Zealand: Reed, 1975

Lake, Deborah. *Smoke and Mirrors*. Stroud: The History Press, 2009

Laxon, W. A., Farquhar, I. J., Kirby, N. J. And Perry, F. W. *Crossed Flags*. Gravesend: World Ship Society, 1997

Mackenzie, S. S. *The Australians at Rabaul*. Queensland: University of Queensland Press, 1987

Madsen, Chris. *The Royal Navy and German Naval Disarmament 1942 – 1947*. London. Frank Cass Publishers, 1998

Manningham, William. *Wartime Log for British Prisoners*. Ely: Melrose Books, 2005

McLean, Meta. *The Singing Ship*. Sydney: Angus & Robertson Ltd.,1941

Muggenthaler, August Karl. *German Raiders of World War II*. Great Britain, Robert Hale Limited, 1977

Moore, Bob and Fedeorowich, Kent (Ed). *Prisoners of War and their Captors in World War II*. Oxford: Berg, 1996

Noack, Charles H. *Komet 1940 – 1941*. Garden Island, NSW: The Naval Historical Society of Australia Inc.,1997

Owen, Winifred. *Captives and Castaways*. Welling, New Zealand: Price Milburn, 1984

Price, Hugh. *The Plot to Subvert Wartime New Zealand*. Wellington: Royal Victoria Press, 2006

Roberts, David. *HMS Thetis*. Merseyside: Avid Publications, 1999

Rogers, Anna (Ed). *The War Years. New Zealanders Remember 1939 – 1945*.New Zealand: Platform, 1989

Sandbach, Betsy and Edge, Geraldine. *Prison Life on a Pacific Raider*. London: Hodder & Stoughton, 1941

Showell, Jak P. Mallman. *German Naval Code Breakers*. Ian Allan Publishing, 2003

Stearns, Patrick. *Q Ships, Commerce Raiders and Convoys*. Kent: Spellmount Limited, 2004

Sweeney, Edward J. *A Merchant Seaman's Survival.* England: E. J. Sweeney, 1999

Waters, S. D. *Clipper Ship to Motor Liner.* London: The New Zealand Shipping Company Ltd., 1939

Waters, Sydney D. *German Raiders in the Pacific.* Vermont: Merriam Press, 2000

Waters, Sydney D. *Ordeal by Sea.* London: The New Zealand Shipping Company Ltd., 1949

West, Nigel. *GCHQ.* Great Britain: George Weidenfeld & Nicolson Limited, 1986

Weyher, Kurt and Ehrlich, Hans Jurgen. *The Black Raider.* London: Elek Books, 1955

Wilson, H. 'Tug'. *Horses, Huns and Hostesses.* Sussex: The Book Guild Ltd. 1993

Williams, David. *Wartime Disasters at Sea.* Somerset: Patrick Stephens Ltd., 1997

Winter, Barbara. *The Intrigue Master.* Brisbane: Boolarong Press, 1995

Wood-Ellem, Elizabeth. *Queen Salote of Tonga.* Honolulu: University of Hawaii Press, 2001

Woodroffe, Gordon Thomson. *Getaway.* Orewa, New Zealand: Riverside Publications, 1998

Woodward, David. *The Secret Raiders.* Great Britain: William Kimber & Co. Ltd., 1955

Unpublished personal accounts

Ball, Rev. Fr, Ernest. *One Man's War*

Campbell, Angus. *Personal account*

Clothier, Ella. *Sketch of Life and Career*

Collinson, Bill. *Diary*

Ellison, Frank. *Personal account*

Garden, Oscar. *Interview by Eric Tucker*

Golding, Rosalie. *Personal account*

Harden, Billy. *Wartime experiences*

Henriksen, Karl Helmer. *Report of life on Komet*

Jones, Alan Fitzgerald. *Sweeney*

Kingsford, Fred. *Personal account*

Meehan, John. *Wilde Coffee. The story of Carl Leopold Bruno Wilde*

Mundie, Miss Florence E. M. *Personal account*

Sommerville, Geoffrey. *Prisoners of War at Sea*

Taylor, Robin G. *Letter to Capt. Upton*

Upton, Captain Herbert Lionel. *Diary*

Williams, Henry Stuart. *Personal account*

Archives

Archives New Zealand

ACIE8798[EA1] Transport – Raider Activities – Evidence given at Commission of Inquiry on Loss of Certain Vessels by Enemy Action, 1941. 1280pp

National Archives of Australia

A1066:IC45/55/3/19 Internees – Australians abroad. Civilians reported lost on board SS Montevideo Maru

A1608:I31/1/2 Compensation to members of crew of M.V. Rangitane

A1608:J45/1/12 War – 1939. Survivors of German raider – Military service of

A2671:50/1941 Oath taken by survivors of raider attack

A373:11801 Overseas – Shelling of Nauru [Allegations of subversive activity]

A433:1943/2/30 Pt1 Survivors from certain vessels sunk by German raiders landed at Emirau Island

A433:1943/2/30 Pt2 Survivors from certain vessels sunk by German raiders landed at Emirau Island

A472:W2477 Survivors of German raided ships - Promise by

A518:F16/2/2 Attack on Nauru shipping – repatriation of survivors

A5954:531/2 Enemy laying of mines and enemy raider activity in Australian waters. Oath taken by survivors of raider attack

A659:1941/1/452 British passengers from ships sunk by German raiders - Question of granting them passport facilities to resume their journey

A8681:1940/337 Public Relations Bulletin - Sailors from prison ship flown to Melbourne by RAAF - Air Force Officers hear graphic stories of life on raiders

A981:DEF126 War Records. Defence: Raider enemy in the Pacific (incl. shelling of Nauru)

AWM124:4/342 Raiders in the Pacific

B3476/4 Survivors landed at Emirau Island by Japanese raiders

B6121:153M Triadic, Triona, Triaster – Sinking of German AMC's Komet and Orion/Survivor statements

B6121:153R Komata, Holmwood, Rangitane, Ringwood, Vinni (Sinkings) (Chief Officers Statements) (Passengers Statements) (Crews Statements)

BP242/1:Q45055 Pt1 Raiders in the Pacific. [Rescue of survivors]

BP242/1:Q45055 Pt2 Raiders in the Pacific. [Rescue of survivors]

D1976:SB1941/378 Passports belonging to survivors from Emirau Island

MP1049/5:2037/3/93 Leakage of information – allegations of disloyalty at Nauru

MP1174/1:618 Raider - typewritten notes (copies) of personal accounts of survivors, printed report of Commission of Inquiry, interview with ships' officers, officers' diary notes, ship log of MS Vinni

SP106/4:SPCI/4 Survivors of Ships Attacked by Raider

SP109/1:78/12/24 Films taken by the survivors of the Pacific Raider

SP109/3:309/19 Censorship. Release of story and pictures picked up from Emirau Island in 1941

Report on Technical Aspects of the Sinking of HMAS *Sydney* and HSK *Kormoran*. Maritime Platforms Division, DSTO, Victoria, 2009

National Archives

ADM1/19771 German auxiliary cruiser commanded by Admiral Weyher
ADM223/3 Evidence of Armed German Raiders
ADM/273/3 Merchant Ships' signal book
ADM/274/4 Wartime instructions for merchant ships
HW8/48 Raiders 1944

National Maritime Museum

NZS/31/16 Rangitane – Sinking by German raider

Index

L

M

N

O

P

Q

R

S

T

U

V

W

Z